Property of:
Chula Vista Public Library
365 F Street
Chula Vista, CA 91910

RDR
From Scarcity
to Abundance

A Complete Guide to
Parish Stewardship

David M. Ponting

W9-CNB-712

MOREHOUSE PUBLISHING

Copyright © 2005 by David M. Ponting

Morehouse Publishing

P.O. Box 1321,
Harrisburg, PA 17105

Morehouse Publishing

445 Fifth Avenue,
New York, NY 10016
Morehouse Publishing is an imprint of Church Publishing Incorporated.

All rights reserved. No part of this book may be reproduced, stored in a retrieval system, or transmitted in any form or by any means, electronic, mechanical, including photocopying, recording, or otherwise, without the written permission of the publisher.

Cover art: Sandra Ivany/Brand X Pictures/Getty Images
Cover design: Jane Thornton

Library of Congress Cataloguing-in-Publication Data
Ponting, David M.
    From scarcity to abundance : a complete guide to parish stewardship / David M. Ponting.
        p. cm.
ISBN-13: 978-0-8192-2248-0 (pbk.)

1. Stewardship, Christian — Handbooks, manuals, etc. I. Title.
BV772.P58 2006   248'.6—dc22   2005033166

Printed in Canada

06 07 08 09   10 9 8 7 6 5 4 3 2 1

CHULA VISTA PUBLIC LIBRARY

3 3650 01731 3159

From Scarcity to Abundance

Chula Vista Public Library
365 F Street
Chula Vista, CA 91910

RDR

"On behalf of the whole church I want to say thank you to David Ponting for an exceptional book. In a complete and compelling manner he shows us that stewardship can be, and indeed must be, a vibrant and vital ministry in the church. I recommend this book to all without hesitation and only wish it had been available at the beginning of my ministry to assist in this important work in the life of our church" — The Most Rev. Andrew S. Hutchison, Archbishop and Primate.

"*From Scarcity to Abundance* is a refreshing, valuable resource for parishes and dioceses that want to take seriously the challenges and opportunities offered through 'Letting Down the Nets,' the implementation initiative for the Anglican Church of Canada's new strategic plan, 'Serving God's World, Strengthening the Church: A Framework for a Common Journey in Christ, 2005–2010. Its publication comes at just the right moment, as clergy and lay leaders begin to make financial and congregational development an essential priority in the life and work of the church. Dave Ponting's book will go a long way in helping us to achieve the exciting vision of General Synod — a church that is growing in membership, faith, and service in God's world" — The Ven. John M. Robertson, National Gift Planning Officer, General Synod.

"This practical guide takes a positive look at financial stewardship in the life of the church. Writing in a straightforward, easy-to-follow style, Dave Ponting shares his experience and passion for Christian stewardship. A useful addition to the library of any parish!" — The Rt. Rev. M. Philip Poole, Suffragan Bishop of Credit Valley, Diocese of Toronto.

"With a very practical and common sense approach, Dave Ponting outlines necessary foundational understandings and uses case studies, illustrative material, templates, and tools to get at the task of changing stewardship attitudes. His approach including helpful 'how to's' regarding narrative budgeting is a gift. I look forward to recommending this new resource as encouragement for the church to take stewardship seriously" — The Rt. Rev. Dr. Claude W. Miller, Bishop of Fredericton.

I came that they may have life, and have it abundantly.

Jesus of Nazareth (John 10:10)

Like good stewards of the manifold grace of God, serve one another with whatever gift each of you has received.

1 Peter 4:10

Table of Contents

"This excellent work, *From Scarcity to Abundance* by David Ponting, holds many practical lessons and valuable insights for church audiences in the United States as well as Canada. Please note that while The Anglican Church of Canada and Episcopal development and stewardship theologies and methodologies are identical, the gifting and tax laws are somewhat different between Canada and the USA.

For precise information on USA allowable tax deductions and the nuances of planned giving instruments, please contact The Episcopal Church Foundation and/or the Missioner for Stewardship and Development at the Episcopal Church Center, 815 Second Avenue, New York, New York 10017 or 1-800-334-7626."

Glenn N. Holliman
Vice President of Giving Services
Episcopal Church Foundation

Preface

For the past five years I have been the Director of Stewardship and Financial Development for the Anglican Diocese of Niagara. During that time the diocese has undertaken several very positive stewardship initiatives amidst a climate of eroding endowment funds, financially motivated parish closings, divisive external influences that have demanded the church's attention, and the seemingly never-ending pressures on parish budgets. Most of the initiatives I would label as being successful. But I am too close to the situation, and evaluating something as subjective as "success" in stewardship is never easy.

Just as Paul's Letter to the Romans is seen by most scholars to be the culmination and summary of his spiritual journey and theological reflection on his experience of God, so this primer represents the summary of what I have come to understand as some of the keys to unlocking the stewardship puzzle in practical ways that are easily implemented at the parish level.

It is intended as a primer that a clergy person, parish stewardship chair, warden, or student could pick up and use immediately as a blueprint to move forward. Some chapters, where appropriate, have questions for readers to ponder. Combining the answers to all the questions should provide you with sufficient input to do an audit of the state of the stewardship ministry in your parish.

My prayer is that applying some of the suggestions in the book will help demystify the stewardship ministry, bring you clarity, a plan, and ultimately bear fruit that will last.

Grandiose comparisons to Paul aside, each one of his journeys began with one step, each letter with the first word. Let us make a new beginning. For, in fact, you have already begun.

David M. Ponting
Hamilton, Ontario

Acknowledgements

I am indebted to so many for their patient tutelage as I have grown in my understanding of how Christian stewardship fits into my own faith journey. I would like to offer a special word of gratitude to Bishop Ralph Spence for the confidence shown in giving me the opportunity to learn on the job and for time to write this book during my workday.

My ministry has been blessed by working with a very strong Stewardship and Financial Development Committee in the Diocese of Niagara for the past five years. To Joe Asselin, Chub Baxter, Diane Beaman, Ian Chadwick, Fred Gosse, Stan Hatcher, Kim Johnston, Darcey Lazerte, Jim Powell, Malcolm Ramsay, Gordon Reed, Gordon Ross, and Sharon White, whose faithfulness and passion for stewardship have been a constant support and inspiration, thank you. My heartfelt gratitude goes to Jim Newman, past chair of that committee, for his friendship, encouragement, and commitment to the ministry of stewardship, his countless hours of volunteer support of my ministry, and for suggesting this book.

A special thank-you also must go to Karen Nowicki, my administrative assistant throughout my stewardship ministry, for all her hard work, loyalty, and the efficient way she approaches all her tasks, freeing me to do my thing. To all those who have shared their personal stories with me of God's providential care in their lives, and with gratitude to the Reverend Joe Asselin, who, on a two-hour plane flight to a rural ministry conference, witnessed to me and gave me the courage to begin to tithe, thank you.

I would like to thank the members of the ad hoc Ontario Stewardship Network, whose passion for stewardship is an ongoing inspiration; Archdeacon Michael Pollesel for his wonderful contribution of the chapter "Taking Care of the Word: Preaching about Stewardship," and Archdeacon Fred Gosse for sharing the stewardship success story illustrated in the case study in chapter 10. Jeff Pym, Planned Giving consultant of the Evangelical Lutheran Church in Canada, Eastern Synod, has shown me the benefits of the broadening and learning we can derive from our ecumenical partnerships, and helped me discover this important new layer in my ministry.

My thanks to Jim Newman, Gordon Ross, Archdeacon Michael Pollesel, and Canon Michael Karabelas for reviewing this manuscript. I am most appreciative of their constructive comments and feedback.

My thanks, too, to my publisher Robert Maclennan of ABC Publishing, who believed in the importance of a book on Canadian Anglican stewardship and, ultimately, made it a reality.

To Deborah, you are so special to me and such a natural giver. Your love gives me wings to fly. Finally, a word to my two wonderful daughters, Jessica and Samantha. Your support, encouragement, and love are a beacon of light on the Way. You are both awesome young women. I am proud beyond words of what wonderful stewardship you model on a daily basis as you give of your selves to others and utilize your gifts as co-creators of the coming reign of God.

Introduction

At times the ministry of stewardship education and development seems for many of us in the mainline Church like pushing a gigantic boulder uphill. Pushing boulders is great exercise if you have a two-ton "Bobcat," but hard on the back and the heart for mere mortals.

At a recent stewardship forum at Wycliffe College in Toronto I spoke to the assembled divinity students from Trinity and Wycliffe of the typical demands on a finite base of donors in an average parish during the course of a year. This partial list would have to include

- parish annual operating budget support;
- parish Capital Campaigns;
- altar guild, flower fund, and memorial fund requests;
- rector's discretionary fund;
- diocesan short-term Capital Campaigns;
- diocesan campaigns to build endowments in foundations;
- Residential Schools Settlement Fund parish commitments;
- Episcopal Foundation appeals;
- Compass Rose Society Appeals;
- Presiding Bishop's World Relief and Development Fund regular gifts and HIV/AIDS campaign;
- Planned Giving requests;
- diocesan newspaper and *national church newspaper* appeals;
- Theological Students' Fund drives;
- Christmas hamper programs sponsoring families;
- special ministries funding, "Faithworks," organ funds, evangelism, outreach;
- refugee family sponsorship programs in many parishes.

Is it any wonder that people in the pews often lament that all the church ever does is ask for money? Although it may appear as if we are always asking for money, this seemingly long list pales in comparison to

---

From Scarcity to Abundance

the massive volume of direct mail and telephone solicitation requests that most Canadians receive consistently every week of the year from the over 86,000 charities registered in Canada.

On a recent Sunday I was filling in for a colleague as supply clergy in a nearby parish. At the end of the eight o'clock service I was handed all the envelopes. I decided to peruse them and see what amounts were written on the outside of each. The amounts were consistent with what I have found to be not uncommon in Canada. I don't know why, but I continue to be shocked by the number of envelopes each week that have $1.00, $2.00, $5.00 stuffed inside. And I ask myself how we have allowed 1960s gifting levels to remain normative in many places throughout the North American Church.

The most recently available national church statistics tell us that Anglicans in Canada give an average of $710 per year to their parish church. Recent statistics from the Evangelical Lutheran Church in Canada, Eastern Synod, reveal an average gift of $883 per identifiable giver. The Lutheran Eastern Synod estimates that this figure represents giving of approximately 1.5% to 2.0% of income. The sad fact is that wealthier dioceses in the southern part of the country actually pull the Anglican average down with their average givings per household, rather than inflate it.

In our Diocese we estimate that Canadian Anglicans give approximately 1% of their household incomes to parish operating budgets. Our most healthy parishes might find that givings may be around 3% of household income. This pales in comparison to most Christian denominations in Canada. We must find creative ways to push this boulder to the top of the hill. We must ask ourselves, What are the obstacles to change? and, How do we begin the job of overcoming them?

One simplistic answer is that asking for money in the Anglican Church is counter-cultural. I was in a room once with twenty-five Anglicans from across the diocese and, after asking for a show of hands, I discovered that not one of the participants had ever been asked by any branch of the Anglican Church to include the church in their wills. Not one. My committee was flabbergasted. In that one moment, the members of the diocesan stewardship committee found within themselves a passion to create a quality Planned Giving program for the parishes in our diocese.

At that Wycliffe divinity students' forum I made a rather bold comment. I told the students that, if they were not prepared to be proactive and aggressive in their approach to incorporating financial stewardship into their ministries, they might as well walk away from their schooling now and not waste any more time, money, and effort on their studies. I told them that I could predict before they ever started in parish ministry that their ministries would not be successful unless they were willing to make stewardship education a priority.

The good news (and we are in the Good News business) is that necessity is the mother of invention. The patient may at times seem palliative, but the Holy Spirit is at work. Struggling parishes are taking notice. Theological colleges are beginning to make stewardship learning a part of formation for ministry. The people in the pews are concerned as they look around on a Sunday morning and make guesses about who is keeping the parish afloat with their time, treasure, and talent, and reflect on the advancing age of these core givers. There has been a growing realization of the importance of the ministry of financial stewardship in the church, and there seems to be a collective plea coming from parishes to provide the resources to put stewardship on the front burners of parish agendas. Additionally, many parishes are finding success and sharing their stories. Attention to stewardship can and does positively impact on parish life.

The North American church has no shortage of stewardship resources. There are many excellent web sites; *Giving* magazine, published annually by the Ecumenical Stewardship Center, is a top-quality, thoughtful resource, and there are many fine books available to help the stewardship practitioner. This primer is one person's attempt to provide a one-stop, "all-in-one," practical Canadian resource for parish leaders to help demystify the financial stewardship process and help Anglicans reclaim the ministry of stewardship in parishes. It has been designed to be read in its entirety. You may wish to go straight to the sections that cover matters of current concern in your parish. If you do skip ahead, I recommend orienting yourself by reviewing the theological framework discussion in chapters 1 and 11. You can also go to Episcopal church website.

Financial stewardship can and must be reframed. It is not the last job we fill partway through the year as the annual September panic sets in about balancing the operating budget. The ministry of stewardship is a vital, vibrant, critically important ministry in every parish. It lies at the heart of the corporate life of the faith community and is part of the very fabric of our personal spiritual journeys.

A Final Word

Throughout this primer I refer often to the ministry of stewardship. I need to make a point to ease concerns of those who rightly understand that stewardship is about much more than the technical financial development ways we raise money to do ministry. I am the last one who would view stewardship as being primarily about money.

In part 1 I have attempted to set a theological framework for parish stewardship ministry. I strongly believe that part of the parish stewardship team's task is to find teachable moments to help congregants understand how Christian stewardship is an essential part of the fabric of our faith journeys. However, as I leave part 1 and move on to the remaining sections of this primer, my focus changes from the spiritual and theological issues to the practical. It could be argued that the book's subject matter shifts from the spiritual to the practical, and becomes primarily about *financial stewardship*. This shift is intended.

PART ONE

GETTING STARTED

It is a very real and tangible truth of the faith journey that people find fulfilment and joy in the utilization of their spiritual gifts

1

A Theological Framework for the Life of Christian Stewardship

Scriptural Starting Points

Our understanding of the call to be stewards of the gifts of God originates in Genesis. The Genesis story teaches us that everything comes from God and everything belongs to God. We are offered a role in God's creation to be managers or stewards of that creation. Taking care of God's creation includes care for not just ourselves, but for others and the environment. The church can be viewed as one vehicle through which we can exercise our role as stewards of creation. When we offer our time, our talent, our treasure to God, we are taking up our baptismal covenant to be stewards and co-creators with God of a new reality. In church language, we call that reality the coming kingdom of God or the reign of God.

Any understanding of stewardship must begin with an awareness that God is the "Great Giver." To be always giving is an essential part of God's nature. None of us can ever "outgive" God. Consequently, we are not called to extraordinary acts of generosity. However, we are called to be careful and wise stewards of the resources God has given us—not just for a time, but throughout our lives. Since we are created in the image of God, we are meant to be givers.

The Church is a Vehicle

An understanding of the theology of Christian stewardship must also include a theological comprehension of the role of the church as the body of Christ on earth. Each of us stands within a long line of a great communion of saints stretching back to the formation of the early Christian church described in Acts 2. As Anglicans, we are inheritors of a gospel faith within a specific liturgical and cultural tradition. Our traditions are rich in worship, sacrament, fellowship, and service to each other and beyond our faith communities. Throughout the 450-plus-year history of the Anglican Church, each generation has received this gospel tradition and been called to steward it for a time and then pass it on to generations that follow.

Since everything comes from God and everything belongs to God, we are called to be faithful stewards of God's gifts in this age and to pass these gifts on to the church that follows in our footsteps. But we can pass on only what we ourselves have received. When we pass our spiritual gifts on to the church, it is empowered to be Christ in the world. We also have monetary gifts that we can give, to provide the financial resources needed for the ministry of the faith community now, and for the communion of saints that will someday follow us.

The parish church is many things. It is a place of worship, friend-ship, and relationship building, healing, and pastoral care; outreach, inreach, and Christian education. In its many ministries we can view the church as a vehicle for us to exercise Christian stewardship. Of course, there are many other vehicles in the community and globally.

An Invitation to the Abundant Life

Jesus and Money

Jesus regularly warned his audiences that to store up treasure is folly. The gifts that God gives are for use on this earth and cannot be taken with us. The parable of the rich landowner (Luke 12:13–34) who tears down old barns and builds bigger barns to store more goods, though his life is about to be taken from him that very night, is an example of Jesus' teaching. Jesus understood that we worship a God of abundance, and that we must live out of a "spirituality of abundance."

Many of Jesus' miracles reinforced his understanding of the abundant life. The changing of the water into fine wine in John 2 at the Wedding at Cana, the feeding of the five thousand from just a few loaves and fishes, the instructions to the disciples to let down their nets on the other side of the boat, and his vast healing ministry—all point to the abundant life that God desires for all his children.

In John 10:10 Jesus tells the disciples why he came to live among humans. He declares, "I came that they may have life, and have it abundantly." Jesus teaches us that the proverbial cup is not half empty or even half full, but overflowing. That is the way our God has designed creation.

Sadly, Jesus seemed deeply troubled that so many of us lack the eyes to see this. So many people unwittingly live their lives out of a "spirituality of scarcity." This is understandable but so unnecessary. We fear that we will never have enough and worry that, though we are doing fine now, at some point in the future we may be in financial peril. Insecurity reigns. It has ever been thus throughout the history of humanity.

In the story of the Exodus the people cry out for food and lament that they are not back in Egypt, under the chains of slavery but at least with fish and grain and food to fill their stomachs. Exodus 16 tells us that God heard the murmurings of the people and provided quail and then manna from heaven each morning. The people were told to take only what they needed and no more. God guaranteed that there would be enough food each day and that the people would not go hungry. But anxiety and a spirituality of scarcity reigned among the Israelites. Many took more food than they needed for each day, and by the next morning they found that the excess had become corrupted—filled with maggots. In Joshua 5:12 we are told that God kept the guarantee that there would be enough. The manna from heaven ceased only on the day that Israel ate the produce of the first harvest of the Promised Land. God provides!

Theologically we need to come to grips with the knowledge that God gives us what we need. That enough is enough. That the abundance of this earth is not to be hoarded but shared.

Human Anxiety

Certainly, Jesus understood that people are anxious about their personal financial security. But people take a quantum leap in their spiritual faith journeys when they are able to trust that God will provide for them continually—that God has always provided for them in the past and will always do so in the future. In Luke 12:22–24 Jesus addresses this anxiety:

> Therefore I tell you, do not worry about your life, what you will eat, or about your body, what you will wear. For life is more than food, and the body more than clothing. Consider the ravens: they neither sow nor reap, they have neither storehouse nor barn, and yet God feeds them. Of how much more value are you than the birds!

Just a few short verses later Jesus reiterates his point: "For where your treasure is, there your heart will be also." We all understand this truth from the teachings of Jesus in our heads. Do we let it make the journey to our hearts? We have a wonderful opportunity to grow beyond our anxiety to a place where the knowledge of God's abundance overflowing in all our lives creates genuine transformation. Our hearts do not have to remain in bondage to a spirituality of scarcity.

Understanding that God's creation is teeming with abundance for all creates a freedom that can bring a deep inner peace to many Christians. When we have a felt experience of God's abundance and generosity, we can respond only in thanksgiving.

A Word about the Biblical Tithe

The biblical standard for personal financial stewardship is the tithe. It's that simple. The biblical tithe is the standard for all Anglicans. Yet there is a huge resistance to tithing in the Anglican culture. It seems to me that tithing would be a non-issue if we were grounded firmly in a spirituality of abundance. The overwhelming resistance to the tithe illustrates dramatically how far the church needs to move spiritually—how locked in so many of us are to a spirituality of scarcity. Many Anglican clergy will tell you that parishioners' eyes gloss over the minute the subject of tithing is raised. Experience has taught clergy to avoid the term and speak, instead, of gradual increases in proportionate giving. Sadly, in the North American context above the Mason-Dixon line, this is the wisest path forward in almost all parishes.

People Have a Need to Give Thanks to God

As a stewardship minister in your parish, you must fully understand a basic aspect of human nature—people want to make generous acts of thanksgiving to God. They have a deep spiritual need to do this. The biblical record overflows with joy in the hearts of ordinary people finding creative ways to give thanks to God for God's many blessings in their lives.

In the story of the Flood, Noah's first act upon finding dry land and leaving the ark in Genesis 7 is to build an altar to the Lord and make offerings of thanksgiving. When Hannah conceives a long-awaited son in 1 Samuel 1, her joy and ecstasy overwhelm her and she offers the boy Samuel to the Lord for service under the high priest Eli in God's temple. In 1 Chronicles 16 David recaptures the Ark of the Covenant from the Philistines and rejoices as it is carried back into Jerusalem. To the scorn of some, David himself is singing, dancing, and making merry. He throws a great party of thanksgiving to God, "[distributing] to every person in Israel—man and woman alike—to each a loaf of bread, a portion of meat, and a cake of raisins."

Solomon is so overwhelmed with God's many gifts in his life that he undertakes the building of the most magnificent temple of its time, joyfully dedicates it to God, and asks that God might make his home there. People from around the Mediterranean world traveled great distances to marvel at its beauty and grandeur.

In the New Testament, stories abound of people's need to give thanks to God for God's blessings in their lives. In John 9 the man born blind is so thankful that he risks his status as a member of his family and is cast out of his community for testifying on Jesus' behalf before the Pharisees. Joseph of Arimathea has been so affected by Jesus' life and teaching that he donates his family's newly dug tomb for the body of Jesus. In Acts 8 we encounter the story of Philip and the Ethiopian eunuch. The Ethiopian is so overjoyed with the Good News, explained to him by Philip, that in thanksgiving he asks for immediate baptism and goes on his way rejoicing.

Grace, Not Guilt

Any theological framework for stewardship must be grounded in the knowledge that stewardship programs are guided by grace, not guilt. The story of God's abundant care for us is a story of grace. I suspect we could raise much more money if we took the position of some televangelists and fostered guilt in people. Every program should be put under the lens of grace to make sure that there is no element of guilt being fostered in the program.

Questions for Reflection

1. Do you live your life out of a spirituality of abundance or scarcity?

2. Does the persona (corporate personality) of your parish as reflected in recent key discussions and decisions in the life of the parish reveal a spirituality of abundance or scarcity? What signs are indicators of your parish's stewardship persona?

3. If you reflect on your giving patterns and habits, has your giving been motivated by grace or by guilt?

2

Nurturing a Culture of Stewardship in Your Parish

So your parish is a place where personalized talk of money has been taboo for decades. You are probably thinking there is very little you can do to change this culture, and you might secretly admit to being very pessimistic about opportunities for turning this around. The first piece of good news is that scripture is on your side as you take up this task. The Bible contains more than 500 references to prayer, almost 500 references to faith, but there are more than 2,000 references to money and possessions.

Jesus understood that money looms large in ordinary everyday life. He talked about money often. Of the thirty-eight parables told by Jesus in the gospels, sixteen deal with how we handle our money. Jesus said more about money and possessions than about heaven and prayer combined. One out of every six verses in the gospels deals with money or possessions—a total of 288 verses in the four gospels!

In Jesus' greatest teaching (that comes to us in Matthew 5 as the Sermon on the Mount) Jesus reiterates the folly of storing up treasures on earth. He addresses anxiety about financial and physical security in that passage, telling the disciples not to worry. He labels this anxiety that we feel about our own future security, and he prescribes a new way.

There is only one conclusion that can be drawn from these numbers and passages. Jesus believed there was a direct connection between money and our spiritual growth. Talk of money is incarnational. Consider just some of the parables where money has a central role in the story:

- the workers in the vineyard—*a discussion about the seeming unfairness of life;*
- the lost coin—*money as a metaphor for God seeking the lost;*
- the widow's offering—*out of her poverty she gave all she had;*
- the prodigal—*the squandering of an inheritance;*
- the shrewd manager—*wise investing;*
- the rich fool—*the folly of storing up wealth;*
- the rich young man—*an invitation to sell everything and follow Jesus;*
- the unforgiving servant—*forgiven a large debt, he calls in a smaller debt;*
- the rich man and Lazarus—*a call to do charitable works while there is still time;*
- the question about paying taxes—*giving the emperor what is his;*
- the talents—*an invitation to be good stewards of God's gifts.*

Since ancient times money has played a key role in daily living. Money issues loom large in your life. They loom large in your fellow parishioners' lives too. Jesus understood this reality and consistently addressed it head on.

Unfortunately within Anglican church culture, compared to that of other Christian denominations, talk of money is believed to be too personal and bad manners. But perpetuating this taboo is *not* scripturally sound. Too many of us perpetuate this taboo unwittingly, I suspect from a need to avoid conflict. Jesus, who came not to bring peace but a sword (Matthew 10:34), understood the basic dynamics of conflict. It is in conflict that we find transformation. Conflict, when managed faithfully and skilfully to bring about transformation, can be a positive element in a faith community. Jesus, who rarely stood on the side of the status quo, courageously took on the religious establishment to usher in a new way of being.

People of the Story

As Christians, we are a people of the story. From Genesis to Revelation we encounter an unfolding story of God's care for God's people. This story has relevance on three levels—for humanity, for each faith community corporately, and for every individual. It is my belief that, through storytelling, we can do some practical, concrete things to help nurture a culture of stewardship in a parish. This will in turn help individual parishioners understand their personal stewardship as a vital component of their faith journey. My story illustrates this.

Several years ago, before ordination, I was working in the business world with a large multinational advertising agency in downtown Toronto. One morning, as I walked across the familiar parking lot, it occurred to me that I was probably the only one of my peers not driving a luxury car. My mind pondered this, and I got it in my head that I "needed" a BMW320i. I started car shopping, combing area dealerships for a car with the right options and price. Within three weeks I was ready to take the plunge and planned to make the purchase one Saturday.

The day I was going to finalize the deal, I looked in my daytimer and realized that I had committed to help my mother move. She was downsizing from the family home into a condominium townhouse. So there we were on moving day—it was late afternoon, and my mother and I were sitting on the cold basement floor unwrapping household items from the newsprint wrapping paper. All around us were the jetsam and flotsam of the move. Wrapping paper and cardboard boxes were stuffed or piled everywhere. Did you know that movers even wrap rolls of toilet paper?

We were sitting on that cold concrete floor, when my mother asked me a question. She pointed to a pile of furniture that the movers had neatly stacked in a corner. "David," she asked, "would you like that pile of family room furniture?" Even then, as a businessman, I had that recessive clergy gene that hates turning down a freebie. But on thinking about her generous offer, I had to admit that I had no place to put any of the surplus furniture.

It was at that point that God hit me in the middle of the forehead with a Mack truck. "You know," my mom mused, "I'm sixty-five years old and it has just occurred to me that I have spent my entire life accumulating and now I am going to be spending the rest of my life giving things away."

It was like a bolt of insight crashed into me and left my ears smoking. What I had known in my head all along about not storing up treasurers on earth finally journeyed its way down to my heart at thirty-five years of age. I can honestly say that, suddenly, the BMW didn't seem important anymore. Now, years later, I believe that the Holy Spirit was stepping up and leading me through a process of conversion. Within six months I was considering a radical career change, and within nine months I was taking a part-time evening course at seminary. I had reframed the role of money in my life. Or the Spirit had. It was not my doing.

Flash forward to a cold late-January afternoon five years later and I am on a flight to Regina, then driving through a blizzard in rural Saskatchewan to Lumsden for an international conference on rural ministry. I think that, two years earlier, conference participants had assembled together in New Zealand. I got Lumsden. Now, for a boy from the suburbs outside Toronto, Lumsden was hard to find on the map. For those of you who don't know where it is, its winter coordinates are approximately that place on the thermometer where Celsius meets Fahrenheit.

Anyway, I digress. I was travelling to this conference on an airplane with a fellow clergy person from my diocese. His name was the Reverend Joe Asselin. Joe and I got talking about tithing. Joe mentioned that he and his wife, Maureen, had made a decision to tithe and how right it felt for them. I pushed him on the subject, eager to learn the impact that decision had made on their lives. The discussion moved me, and I began shortly after to tithe my salary for the first time in my life.

Six years later I was going through a devastating divorce. In addition to all the grief and mourning that come with such an overwhelming life change, I was preoccupied with issues of money. How was I ever going to be able to provide for my family and myself under very different circumstances? Added to my preoccupation was my guilt over being the staff stewardship person for the diocese and still unable to move beyond worrying about money. I was obsessing over this topic at lunch one day with Jim Newman, a friend who at that time was also chair of the diocesan stewardship committee. Jim is a very wise man, and he said something that day I will never forget.

"Dave, hasn't God taken care of you so far?" I had to admit that God has. "Well, what makes you think God is going to stop taking care of you and your family now?" Once again I was caught in the headlights of that Mack truck with no room to maneuvre. God had gained my attention.

These are but a few chapters in what I have come to view as my own personal stewardship story. There are others and, by God's grace, many chapters yet unwritten. As I have reflected on this and talked to other committed Christians around the diocese, I have come to realize that we all have a very personal and sacred stewardship story. Imagine the impact on a parish if you could create a culture where even a few committed people were encouraged to reflect on, and share, their own sacred stewardship story. I believe this is achievable.

As parish stewardship champion, you can do several things to nurture this culture. The first thing you must do is to reflect on your own unique stewardship story. Take the time to write down the times in your life when you have felt God's providential care for you. At a diocesan seminar, a priest in our diocese told the group of the time she was on vacation in Europe and caught unawares with no money by a four-day bank holiday. Perfect strangers took care of her, fed her, housed her, and ministered to her, displaying their generous hospitality. For her, it was a transformative experience, and she has come to view this time as part of her own sacred story. She believes God taught her a valuable lesson about the role of money in her life.

My point is simple. If you reflect on these things, you *will* discover your own sacred story. As parish leaders, having done this spiritual work, we can then encourage others to do the same. Ideas abound. You can make reflection on a sacred stewardship story (yours or another's) the main agenda item of a parish council meeting; have lay people tell their story during sermon time; use the parish newsletter to run a series of sacred stories; make exploring individual sacred stories the focus of a Lenten study. The ideas can extend as far as your imagination.

We Grow in Community

As I reflect on my own sacred stewardship story, and as others tell me theirs, I have come to see one constant ingredient. If you look at the "chapters" in my story, you'll notice some principal characters. My mother, Joe Asselin, and Jim Newman have had a part to play. The work that the Spirit was doing in me was happening within the context of community. I was not struggling with these weighty issues alone. I was in Christian community where two or more are gathered. The lesson that my priest friend learned traveling through Europe occurred in the context of the hospitality of a community of strangers, come together to aid her in her time of need.

It is in the context of community where you journey with the people of your parish. The faith community models, supports, and holds each member accountable for the maintenance of its joint mission and core values. It is in community where we can call others to join us in living out our baptismal ministries by recognizing and identifying spiritual gifts, empowering their use, and giving thanks for the fruit these gifts bear in the lives of others. It is in community that you gift others by sharing your sacred story, modeling the hope within you, and inviting them to make intentional Christian stewardship a part of their faith journeys.

Two Distinct Components of Parish Stewardship

In appreciating the role of the parish stewardship committee, we can consider its somewhat dualistic nature. I have found it helpful to think of parish stewardship ministry as having two very distinct components.

One element is to put in place the widespread use of logistical tools to promote self-examination by individuals. Self-examination is essential as we invite parishioners to contemplate how they will give thanks to God with their time, talents, and money. There are many tools available for this process, and they will be discussed in the next section of this primer. This job requires administrative and executional skills, strong attention to detail, and the ability to make follow up a priority.

Creating an environment where self-examination takes place with regularity is a vital component, necessary to nurturing a culture of stewardship. In creating this environment you are, in fact, issuing a quality invitation to self-examination. You put out a quality invitation, and then the level of response is really up to the Holy Spirit. Experience indicates that, when people make dramatic behavioral shifts in their Christian stewardship, it is often due to a process of conversion that takes place as stewardship becomes part of the very fabric of one's personal faith journey.

The good news is that the fruits of a regular program encouraging self-examination are measurable. There are some obvious tools to determine progress, such as average annual gift per household, increase in number of identifiable givers, increase in ministries with solid volunteer support, increase in use of pledge cards or pre-authorized payment plans.

Companions on a Journey

The second element is less concrete and much harder to evaluate its progress. The other job of the parish stewardship team is to become companions on a journey. It is the journey from scarcity to abundance, a journey we are all on. It is the job of stewardship education. It is the task of giving people a new lens with which to view their lives. This is the lens through which we can see God's abundant care for all creation. Our job is to give people a theological framework and to model Christian stewardship in our lives. It is to create a parish climate where the sharing of personal stories is normative and inspirational. Bishop Claude Payne of the Episcopal Diocese of Texas writes,

> Although spiritual development is not painless, it is deeply
> rewarding and enormously satisfying precisely because it
> represents a repudiation of false gods and impotent altars—a
> process of rededication and realignment that is not without
> suffering. Yet the pain of abandoning false gods is nothing in
> comparison to the joy of embracing the real God.[1]

Payne argues that there is a spiritual hunger in North America that needs satisfying, as people discover that the false gods they have been chasing do not satisfy. This is the essence of the journey from scarcity

---

1 Bishop Claude Payne and Hamilton Beazley, *Reclaiming the Great Commission* (San Francisco: Jossey-Bass Publishing, 2000), p. 11.

to abundance. We learn that the false gods of wealth and materialism we have been worshipping bring no solace or peace. Accumulation of material goods does not make our insecurities and fears of scarcity vanish. We all hunger for another way. Stewardship education points to a way that satisfies this hunger and supports your fellow congregants on their journey.

You may wonder if you are competent to be a companion on such a journey. It seems to me that, if you have struggled with your own sacred story, and if you are a generous giver—whether of your time or your treasure—then you are qualified to take on this task. No one is on a straight-line journey from scarcity to abundance. I know I oscillate back and forth between the two, sometimes to the extreme. The goal we must keep in front of us is to be on the journey—to have the courage to embark on a life of regular self-examination that is unafraid to look at the false gods in our lives.

A Reflection on Leadership and Nurturing a Culture of Stewarship

In the spring of 2000 the Diocese of Niagara was in the middle of an $8-million diocesan-wide Capital Campaign. It was, in essence, not one campaign but 114 small parish campaigns running simultaneously across the diocese. As Director of Stewardship and Financial Development for the diocese, my job was to work with the professional fund-raising consultants to ensure that all parishes participated and maximized their opportunities for success. As part of my duties, I assisted the assessment of donor prospects, trained committee members and visitors, preached sermons on why the campaign was going to empower local ministry, and generally assisted parishes in whatever way I could. The professional consultants, who were not well versed in Anglican church culture, often called on me when they hit a roadblock of parish resistance with no seeming way forward.

One Tuesday evening I was invited to a small urban parish in this troubleshooting capacity. It was a parish council advisory board meeting, and over twenty of the core members of the parish were in attendance. The parish seemed always to be struggling, and the campaign, according to the rector, required energy they lacked. The problem was laid out very early in the meeting. The campaign was so unpopular that the parish rector and wardens had been unable to recruit even one person to make the face-to-face visits the campaign required. What could they do, they wondered aloud, to motivate people to visit?

I looked around the room and began to ask questions about the extent of their involvement with the parish and the length of their association with this particular faith community. I listened in wonder to the sacred stories of how proud they were of their association with the parish and how important the parish had become in their lives.

After hearing their stories I started to pack up my laptop briefcase to leave.

"Where are you going?" they asked me, with surprise in their voices. "We thought you were here to help us."

I said to them, "You don't need me. You have a crisis in this parish far more important than your participation in this diocesan campaign."

People looked at one another puzzled and somewhat annoyed. "What do you mean we have a crisis here?"

I stood behind my chair with my suit coat flung over my shoulder and said that I believed they had a crisis of leadership in the parish. The room buzzed in protest to my intentionally contentious comment. When the din settled, I asked them how many of the parish council present that night had agreed to be visitors in the campaign.

No one responded. For a few people, the light went on.

I told them that, until the people who understood themselves as parish leaders started acting like leaders, I believed the parish would continue to tumble from crisis to crisis. To my surprise, they didn't reach for the tar and feathers and chase me down the street. "Sit down and talk with us," the rector said in earnest.

We had a long conversation that night about leadership, and what it means to accept the gift and responsibility of leadership in the church. We talked about the need for leaders to model stewardship of the gifts of God for the rest of the congregation. Many of the ideas that came out were not mine. That evening, we began to move forward.

It seems to me there is a leadership void in many of our parishes. I am not referring specifically to clergy or laity, but talking about leadership in general. Nowhere is this void so gaping as in the area of our Christian stewardship. Being a Christian is risky. I know it is not easy to talk to others about investing their money and precious leisure time in the ministry of a parish. I know some people will get angry when we broach the subject, and we will from time to time find ourselves in situations that are very uncomfortable. But it costs money to do ministry, and many Anglicans are not giving enough of their treasure to fund that ministry. We need to take the risk of faith to talk about this reality. We need to search the way we do things and give people better reasons to give.

In many places the North American Anglican/Episcopalian Church is in crisis. There are complex problems that are both local and systemic. For most of my current ministry I have done a lot of guest preaching in the many parishes in our diocese. Most Sunday mornings, as I drive home, I sadly reflect that, if I had a choice to worship in the place where I had just preached, I probably would not. Often it seems as if the parish is either dead or palliative. But it is not like that every Sunday. Some Sundays I drive home wishing I could be the rector of that particular parish. Wishing I could be captain of a ship of people not afraid to try new things, not afraid to experiment and fail, not afraid to learn and relearn over and over again what it means to be the body of Christ in a changing world.

Let us populate our stewardship committees with people who are true givers. Givers of their time, their talents, and their treasure. People not afraid to lead. People who grasp that leading means modeling by example. I believe we need a new understanding of what being a leader in the Anglican Church means at the parish level. If someone wants to be a parish leader, they need to do some regular prayerful self-examination of the state of their discipleship. A leader must be tithing or making progress toward increased proportionate giving. A leader must lead.

Do all the members of your parish council or vestry give generously of their time and talent? Do they tithe 10% of their free time? Do they give concrete support to the goal of 80% of the givers on the parish list being on a pre-authorized payment plan? Have they considered a Planned Gift to the church? Are they prepared to sign a joint statement from the parish council to the parish at large indicating and modeling the fundamental principles of stewardship?

I don't think we should expect anything less. These are expectations for all who would call themselves followers of Jesus Christ. Sure it's risky. But it seems to me at this season in the life of our church that, if we aren't prepared to take large risks, we shall perish as an institution. At the very least, regardless of whether we personally care about the institution of the church, to shy away from considered, prayerful risk is to model a lack of trust in the Holy Spirit and to deny the possibility of the wonderful, unexpected, exciting adventure the Creator holds out as a promise to us all.

A Parish Stewardship Manifesto

If you and I were to catalogue the ministries that make up the fabric of parish life, we'd probably come up with similar lists, including worship, pastoral care, outreach, fellowship, Christian education, and evangelism. For many, stewardship would probably not be top of mind on such a list. Yet each of these essential components of parish ministry involves a core understanding that as disciples we are, first and foremost, stewards of the gifts of God that have been entrusted to our care. We are stewards of the Word, Sacraments, and each other. I have come to see that every sermon I have ever preached is really a stewardship sermon because, at its root, every sermon is calling the congregation to reflect on how we respond to God for God's abundant blessings in our lives. The Christian life is a stewardship life.

Is this understanding at the core of life in your parish? Consider the following parish stewardship manifesto. Nurturing a culture of stewardship includes overt intentionality around declaring the parish a stewardship parish. In my view, stewardship must have primacy among the core values of a faith community. The following stewardship manifesto provides a model that can be adapted, adopted, and communicated to the parish where it is held up as the ideal.

Desired Outcomes for Parish Stewardship Programs

The following list of outcomes is adapted with permission from a list that the Evangelical Lutheran Church in Canada created for its national stewardship initiative. The adaptations to the list are meant to reflect possible stewardship outcomes that a parish could seek to aspire to. Consider playing with it and customizing it for your parish, and then sharing it widely in the parish on your web site, or in your newsletter and bulletins.

A. The parish will articulate and embrace an understanding of the integral role of stewardship in the life of the community that reflects the gospel.

As a result,

1. The congregation will model the behaviors of faithful stewardship.

2. The congregation and leadership will explore and encourage faithful stewardship year-round through learning, worship,

and personal faith formation, especially as it relates to Christian stewardship.

3. Members will participate generously in congregation and community life through personal involvement, prayer, a steadily growing level of financial support, and a lifestyle of justice and compassion for all creation.

4. The parish will communicate clearly about the vision and opportunities for mission and ministry in the church and the wider community.

5. This church will assist members in discerning their spiritual gifts and encouraging them to commit their time to the greatest effect and benefit to the individual and the church.

6. The church will practice good stewardship by receiving financial and in-kind gifts graciously, using them prudently and to maximum effect according to the directions of givers, and accounting for their use with transparency and openness.

B. Parish members will attempt to grow as stewards of God's creation in all aspects of our lives: personal relationships, home, congregation, community, church, and the world, including the care and use of time, money, abilities, vocation, health, well-being, and the environment.

1. In their daily lives, members will reflect increased awareness of God's call to live intentionally as Christian stewards.

2. Members' lives will show evidence of generosity of spirit, joy, personal wholeness, and a greater sense of justice and compassion.

3. The per capita percentage giving of members to the parish will increase annually as measured by an increase in average gift per identifiable giver.

From Scarcity to Abundance

4. An increasing number of members will make regular gifts beyond weekly offerings to the congregation to church institutions, endowments, and foundations, and will designate Planned Gifts to the Episcopalian Church through the financial vehicles available.

By intentionally promoting stewardship as a core parish value, and by encouraging people to discover and share their stories, you can, over time, nurture a culture of stewardship in your parish. It is a wonderful gift you can give your congregation.

Questions for Reflection

1. Reflect on your own sacred stewardship story.

2. What is the sacred story of your parish's stewardship ministry over time to your local community?

3. How does your commitment of time, talent, and treasure reflect where you are in your spiritual journey?

4. Does the preaching in your parish reflect Jesus' attitudes toward the incarnational nature of money?

5. How did you find yourself reacting emotionally to the reflection in this chapter on the nature of leadership in the church?

6. How does the parish stewardship manifesto reflect the core values of your parish? How would you modify it for your parish?

3

Personal Money Management

The Elephant in the Room

This may well be the shortest chapter in this book. It may also well be one of the most important. There is an elephant in the room whenever I talk about stewardship with my fellow Anglicans. That elephant has a name, and that name is Poor Personal Money Management. Often I am acutely aware that, when I preach about Christian stewardship, more than half of my listeners are unskilled in issues of personal money management, never having enough money to meet the bills at the end of the month.

For me, writing a chapter on personal money management is like running with my eyes closed. I would be consumed by guilt if I were to hold myself up as an example of someone who is getting it all right. I am on a journey, getting better I hope, but with a long way to go. Sound personal money management is essential to living the life of the Christian steward. For most people this is where the pedal hits the metal. As stewardship ministers in our parishes we have an opportunity to hold out an ideal for parishioners. The key is to do so with integrity—owning up to our experience, while articulating our hopes, wishes, and dreams for stewarding our personal financial futures.

It would be a genuine and practical help to the stewardship committee in most parishes to invite a carefully selected personal financial planner to hold workshops on the basics of personal financial planning. My interest here is primarily to identify a serious pastoral need and call parishes to creative solutions, not to promote a particular resource or recommend access to our parishes for personal financial planners motivated essentially by a desire to solicit new business. With that caveat duly noted, the General Synod of the Anglican Church of Canada has some excellent resources available to all clergy across the Canadian church through the Employee Assistance Program (EAP).

These General Synod resources include an exceptional paperback called *Money 101: Every Canadian's Guide to Personal Finance* by Ellen Roseman. The author's stated goal is to demystify money and help you master your personal finances. It covers everything from keeping track of your spending, finding ways to cut back spending, how and when to use credit, how to save, how to invest, retirement planning, and tax planning. It is simple and easy to understand.

The EAP program plan also publishes several tracts on personal financial planning, debt control, budgeting, bargain shopping, saving for children's education, overcoming compulsive spending habits, and many other financial topics. These resources are definitely worth looking into and available from the General Synod pension and benefits office.

A book entitled *Three Simple Rules* by Theo A. Boers provides an uncomplicated approach to understanding finances. Written from a Christian perspective, this resource focuses on helping the reader to apply sound personal financial management principles in their daily lives. It's a great book for your church library, a Lenten study evening, or as a gift to all the young couples and singles in your congregation. You can order the book by sending $5.00 US with your name and address to Three Rules, 2600 Five Mile Rd NE, Grand Rapids, MI 49525 or download absolutely free at <http://www.threerules.org>.

Another helpful book for personal financial planning is called *The Millionaire Next Door* by Thomas J. Stanley and William D. Danko. It provides a simple recipe for financial planning for the future, and should be required reading for all newlyweds who find themselves locked in an acquisitive mindset, determined to quickly accumulate the four-bedroom house, the two cars, and the big-screen television. The authors studied people who had a net worth of at least one million dollars, and found some very interesting things to be true about them.

The subjects studied were primarily first-generation millionaires who acquired their money through employment earnings. But they rarely spent it. Forget the foreign luxury cars, monster homes, and expensive decadent vacations. They almost never spent a dime they didn't really have to. Many were reported to have made comments like, "Why buy a BMW or Mercedes when you can get to the same place in a Chevy?" These people were still doing things and enjoying life; they were not curmudgeonly hermits.

One caveat, however. In its recipe for financial success, this book does *not* encourage charitable giving; this is, of course, the key limitation of its usefulness as a Christian teaching tool. Its primary benefit to stewardship ministers is the way it lays out the need for "a good offense" and "a good defense" in our personal money management. All of these books may be found at your local library, bookstore, or through a Google search on the Internet.

Teachable Moments

The emphasis on almsgiving in Lent provides an opportunity to run a Lenten series on personal financial planning. We probably underutilize the potential power of our parish newsletters by not using them to teach subjects such as these. Addressing this topic can be a wonderful gift for your parishioners. Wouldn't this be a positive life-giving way for the church to be more relevant and proactive pastorally in people's lives? We know intuitively that many of our parishioners are struggling mightily with their personal habits around money. Yet without providing teaching in this area, we may inadvertently be complicit in perpetuating a cycle of poor financial stewardship and prolonging deep-seated anxiety and pain around unresolved and ongoing inept management of money and the complications that result.

As Christian stewards we believe that our personal money habits are reflective of our spiritual journey. Perhaps we have been letting parishioners down by our own anxieties and perceived shortcomings on this subject. Many people don't "get it right." I would submit that stewardship education for personal money management is both appropriate and necessary, and also theologically and pastorally sound. We have the materials. Many parishes have other human resources within the congregation to make this kind of education a reality. Lent provides the perfect teachable moment.

If I were running a personal financial-planning stewardship program in my parish, I could think of no better book to use as a theological cornerstone and starting place than Richard Foster's 1981 masterpiece, *Freedom of Simplicity*. Although several years old and partly out of date, the book holds out a new way of being that is a clarion call to all Christians if we are truly to embrace our stewardship of the planet and its resources, our gifts, and ourselves. In this handbook to creating a more human style of living, Foster guides readers on the simple path toward finding God by learning to listen, to give, to show compassion, and to accept what they already have.

I urge parish stewardship teams seriously to consider this element of stewardship education. It is easy to dismiss, but I believe it has been ignored in the past at our peril.

Questions for Reflection

1. How capable a steward of your own personal finances are you? Do you worry a lot about money and issues of financial security? What do you need to do to correct this problem?

2. Does a lack of personal success in this area intimidate you and keep you from addressing this topic with parishioners?

3. Who in your parish might be a resource to provide this pastoral service to parishioners?

From Scarcity to Abundance

4

Taking Care of the Word: Preaching about Stewardship

Michael Pollesel

Millions of people down through the centuries have sat, stood, or dozed through millions of sermons. Some of them may have been graciously short and to the point. Others may have been painfully long and hard to grasp. A few may actually have been memorable or even spellbinding, and may have contributed to the hearer's life and journey in a meaningful way.

I hope that this chapter will be helpful to those charged with the sometimes frightening, sometimes exciting, and always daunting ministry of preaching. I don't pretend that it will answer all your stewardship preaching challenges. Many people, however, don't have a well of experience to draw from when preaching about stewardship. It is my hope that the chapter will suggest a framework, a place to start, and some ideas for stewardship preaching. You will develop these ideas as you integrate them with your personal stewardship journey and, in time, you will find your own voice.

We'll begin by considering a definition of stewardship and the task of the preacher. Then we'll look at how these two topics come together through the ministry of stewardship preaching. I plan to share with you a very simple formula for preparing a sermon from a stewardship perspective. At the end of the chapter, I'll offer some thoughts on the ministry of stewardship preaching. Not only is there a teaching aspect in this kind of preaching; there is also a prophetic aspect that calls for the personal transformation and conversion in all areas of individual and corporate life.

God's Dream

> When long before time and the worlds were begun,
> when there was no earth and no sky and no sun,
> and all was deep silence and night reigned supreme,
> and even our Maker had only a dream.[2]

Archbishop Desmond Tutu, with his characteristic flair for words, puts it this way:

> Dear Child of God, before we can become God's partners, we must know what God wants for us. "I have a dream," God says. "Please help me to realize it. It is a dream of a world whose ugliness and squalor and poverty, its war and hostility, its greed and harsh competitiveness, its alienation and disharmony are changed into their glorious counterparts, when there will by more laughter, joy, and peace, where there will be goodness and compassion and love and caring and sharing."[3]

My understanding and interpretation of the creation story leads me to understand that God's "dream," God's plan for all the created order, is that there shall be *shalom*. In other words, not simply "peace," but a healthy kind of well-being, harmony, and communion among

---

2   Peter Davison, *When Long Before Time,* hymn 307, found in *Common Praise* (Toronto: Anglican Book Centre, 1998).

3   Desmond Tutu, *God Has a Dream* (New York: Doubleday, 2004), 19–20.

humans, as well as between humans and the rest of the created order, and between humans and God.

Some may argue that this interpretation of the creation story pays no attention to Genesis 3, which speaks about the Fall. They would remind us that we are living in the aftermath of the Fall, and that we always need to keep this in mind. While I agree that the Fall is part of the Story, I would also argue that it comes after the initial creation story, and therefore ought not to have the same weight, or be on an equal footing with the primary story.

The story tells us that each and every one of us is a steward. God has entrusted the care of everything there is to us. And when we embrace this role, when we live it out, we are in essence working in partnership with God, doing our part in helping to make God's dream a reality. For me, this means that preaching can be seen as the act of speaking God's dream as revealed in the words of scripture, and holding various aspects of that dream up for examination as we bring it alongside various situations in our contemporary world and our own lives. Preaching can become a kind of dialogue between these two resource materials—God's dream and our situation.

On the one hand, the words we read and hear in scripture help us catch glimpses of God's dream for us and for all of the created order. On the other hand, our newspapers are filled with all the "stuff" of everyday life. We read in the news about people who may be suffering because of some natural calamity, or an injury caused by other human beings. We read about people who may be happy because of something that happened to them, or in which they played a role. We read about births, accidents, deaths, and all the other events that go on in the day-to-day lives of people on our planet.

The preacher's task is to make links between these two texts— God's dream in scripture and our lives in the news—to draw comparisons, to point out discrepancies, to establish links, and to uncover insights that may be hidden just below the surface. This may be how things currently are, but this is not what God's dream for the situation might be. If we allow for, and work with, God's dream of shalom, for healing and reconciliation in the situation, then the dream can renew our lives.

This chapter isn't meant to be a formal discourse on preaching. So let's dispense with terms such as expository or doctrinal preaching, topical or textual preaching, or any of the other classical names that might be used in a classroom setting. Instead, I would like us to consider what a sermon is meant to accomplish. What is the goal of a sermon? What would cause a listener to say, "That was a *good* sermon"?

A sermon can be educational. The preacher offers certain teachings, for example, some facts about a given historical practice during a particular biblical time, or about something happening in our own world, whether close at hand or in a faraway region of the globe. A sermon can also address a given theme or topic, such as How do human beings show love for one another, or What does scripture have to say about God's love for creation?

Most of us will have been subjected to what could properly be called harangues from the pulpit, sermons whose aim was to make us feel guilty, sorry, or ashamed for not doing enough or for doing "wrong" things. Hopefully, the days of such fire and brimstone sermons are long gone. Most people reject or recoil from this type of approach. Better that we encourage, motivate, and inspire others by combining a gospel of grace with a response that comes out of thankfulness and appreciation.

Preachers do no one a service if they fail to spend time preparing. They do the Word in scripture a disservice, by not taking the time to let it soak through various layers of thought and prayer, along with other layers of scholarly explanation and interpretation. They do the people in the pews a disservice by not offering a quality product, to which they are entitled. They do themselves a disservice by thinking they speak a word from God to God's people.

Let me also say that longer isn't necessarily better. The quality of a sermon doesn't improve the longer it takes to deliver. Even the best wines will begin to loose their taste and flavor after being aired too long!

A "Good" Sermon

Having said a few words about some characteristics that I believe make for a less-than-adequate sermon, let's think briefly about what goes into making a "good" sermon. People sitting in the pews, or on the chairs, need to be respected. We need to honour their intelligence and their time commitment. So I would suggest that a good sermon should not be too long. There's a saying we've often heard: "If the preacher can't say it in twelve or so minutes, it's not worth saying."

I have suggested that a sermon should be built around two major points—the Word in scripture, and a situation in today's world—and that it should bring these points together, allowing them to intersect and interact with each other, to speak to each other, to question and challenge each other. This suggests a third point: bringing into effect God's dream, making God's dream real. A good sermon might simply hold the two points, the two focuses, side by side, asking the listeners what they can do to correct the imbalance, and ending with an invitation to help make God's dream come true in a particular situation.

Consider, for example, a vision of God's dream presented in one of the many stories beginning "the kingdom of heaven is like...." What particular aspects of God's dream does Jesus present in such a story? How does the story speak to a particular situation in our own society, such as the increasing gap between those who "have" and those who "have not"?

What other ingredients go into making a sermon good? I assume that readers will be familiar with many of these other ingredients, such as style of delivery and effective communication; proper use of examples and illustrations; appropriate personal anecdotes and comments; suitable inclusion of humor; adequate research for facts and figures; a well-crafted and thought-out structure, in which there is a beginning, a middle, and an end. There are many good books available to help people study all the various aspects of preaching.

One final thought. A sermon will be good if the preacher believes in what she or he is saying. To make what might sound like an obvious point: the preacher must believe in the product and needs to come across as such. From a marketing perspective, the preacher is selling a product. Belief in the product will go a long way to convince listeners that it is a worthwhile product.

Having considered what makes a good sermon, let's now turn our attention to the other topic in this chapter—stewardship—and begin by exploring some definitions.

Stewardship

If you flip through any book or magazine article with "stewardship" in its title, or do an Internet search for the word, you may be surprised at how many different definitions you will find. The words "steward" and "stewardship" have as wide a usage, and maybe even a healthier understanding, outside church circles as within. There is a plethora of stewardship organizations and groups dealing with the care of land, animals, and natural resources. These secular groups generally make no claims to religious belief, and yet their principles have very deep roots in our Judeo-Christian heritage.

Within Christian circles we seem to have become stuck on the narrower definition of stewardship. As a result, "stewardship" seems to have become a code word for "money." At least, that is how many people seem to interpret it. Of course, there are other definitions out there. According to The Ecumenical Stewardship Center, a group with which I am affiliated, "Christian stewardship is grateful and responsible use of God's universe in the light of God's purpose as revealed in Jesus Christ. Christian stewards, empowered by the Holy Spirit, commit themselves to conscious, purposeful decisions." (See <http://www.stewardshipresources.org/html/who_mission.html>.)

Others have offered shorter, but similar definitions, like "Stewardship is everything I do after I say 'I believe' " (John Westerhoff III); "stewardship is the generous offering of our time, talents, and treasure"; and "stewardship is joyfully giving back to God a portion of what God has given us." All of these are good and valid ways of defining what we mean by stewardship. They acknowledge that God is the creator, that God is the owner of all, that what we have is not really ours but has been entrusted to us, that we are to care for it, and that our response ought to be one of joyful thanksgiving.

My own formal definition of stewardship began to take shape a number of years ago when I was volunteer chaplain for a week at Camp Hyanto, our diocesan camp. Having been newly appointed to the office of Stewardship Education Coordinator in our diocese, I decided I ought to devote the chaplain's time with the children that week to an exploration of stewardship. And so we began "in the Big Inning," as my former bishop used to say. We started with a look at the story of creation. We discovered that stewardship has its roots right there, in the opening chapters of the Book of Genesis—God creating, God declaring all to be good, God handing the care of everything into human hands.

For me, "taking care" is as valid a definition for stewardship as any other. God gave all into our care. There is nothing for which we are not to care. Implied in this definition is God's generosity. God has given *all* to us. Our God is a God of infinite abundance. Implied in this definition is the call to nurture, to help develop and grow, everything that God has entrusted to us. We need to remember the stories that Jesus told. He reminded his listeners that God's dream included the desire to expand, to multiply, to help grow gifts and talents entrusted to one or other individual.

Seen from this particular perspective, the story of creation has very broad and wide-ranging implications. If we accept that God has generously given all into our care, then our primary role in life is to follow God's example. Being made in the image of a generous giver, we can spend our lives learning, and trying to put into practice, what it means to "take care" in a generous manner.

Our primary caregivers teach us to take care of ourselves (we are, after all, the temple of the Holy Spirit). As we grow, we learn from them and others how to care for others, how to care for material things, how to care for "this fragile earth, our island home" (*The Book of Alternative Services,* 201). We learn that taking care involves much more than simply having food, clothing, and shelter. We learn that taking care also involves practices and beliefs to which we have been exposed and introduced. In short, we learn that taking care involves every aspect of our lives, from taking care of ourselves, to taking care of our relationships with others, to taking care of created things, to taking care of what some might consider abstract ideas and thoughts, including the gospel message.

If it has been our good fortune to grow up in an environment that has nurtured our growth and development, we also learn how to be thankful. We learn that much of what we have has not been earned, but freely and lovingly given. We learn that there are many things that we can't get, even if we had more possessions or money than we actually have. It is on this foundation that solid, practical, day-to-day, real-life stewardship can be practiced. And, it is from this foundation that stewardship preaching can grow.

Stewardship Preaching

Let me begin with a very bold statement. There is no Sunday in our church calendar when one or more of the appointed scripture passages cannot be interpreted as speaking to us from a stewardship perspective. To prove this point, I have gone through the three-year Revised Common Lectionary cycle of gospel readings and have written two-line stewardship reflection for each.[4] What does such an approach accomplish?

First, it gets us away from the idea that a once- or twice-a-year sermon on money is all there is to stewardship. It also helps preachers and people begin to appreciate that stewardship, while most definitely involving money, also involves a great deal more. It helps move us along the path to recovering a broader, more holistic understanding of stewardship. At one of the first workshops I ever attended during a stewardship conference, the presenter reminded us that growth comes more easily, and with superior results, when there is a regular and gentle rainfall rather than a sudden torrential downpour!

A Formula

I believe that most people who have had some experience preaching will have developed a process or formula for crafting their weekly homiletic offering. However, even before using such a formula, they need to have a foundation to build on. A preacher can lay such a foundation by answering the following questions for him or herself (and this need not be a long, involved process):

- What do I believe is God's purpose in creation?

- How would I describe God's purpose?

- What do I understand the purpose of Jesus to be in that process?

- How and where do I fit into all of this?

---

4 These can be found online on Niagara diocesan web site at <http://www.ontario.anglican.ca>. Select resources then scroll down to "Sunday by Sunday: Reflections on Stewardship, based on the RCL gospels," and click on the appropriate year.

Here, for example, is how I answer these questions. As I've said, I describe God's purpose in creation as bringing God's dream into reality. God's dream begins to come true as the drama of creation unfolds. I regard Jesus as the pinnacle of creation. His role is central to the Christian faith. What I bring to this unfolding drama is my particular and individual self. My role is not only to emulate and follow Jesus but, in doing so, to assist in making God's dream come even just a little closer to reality.

In this section I would like to walk you through a formula that you can use when preparing your sermons from a stewardship perspective. I believe that, when we are look for something, we tend to see it more easily when we have focused our eyes to look for it, or when we have trained our minds to think about it. For example, someone involved in sports will see other aspects of life through a sports lens. They might talk about stepping up to the plate, or being in a sudden-death situation. If we look for references to stewardship, we will be more likely to see them.

So, the essential ingredient in this formula is to be reading scripture and looking at everyday situations through a stewardship lens. A word of caution: we need to be careful not to stretch the limits of credulity, or succumb to the temptation to see things that aren't really there.

How do we develop a stewardship lens? By asking ourselves questions such as these: Is this scripture passage an example of how God or Jesus is acting as a steward? What exactly has been entrusted to us? Is there an indication of compassion, sensitivity, forgiveness, or understanding? Is creation mentioned or involved? Are relationships mentioned or involved? Do we see a connection or dependency between the rest of creation and ourselves? Is there some reference in this particular passage to taking care? Is there some indication of generosity in this passage?

In looking at a given contemporary situation, we can ask many of the same questions, as well as others. For example, would a prophetic stance in a given circumstance be called for? Is social justice or advocacy something that involves helping to make God's dream more real in this or that instance? Can I legitimately challenge where and how people spend their money, their time, or their skills and talents in a given situation?

And with our newspapers in hand, so to speak, we can ask: What kinds of messages do I get from the culture and society I live in, with regard to taking care, with respect to generosity, about my own worth and well-being? I am certainly not the first to point out that we live in a consumer-oriented society, which seems to place more value on goods and services than on people. Many times a day we are subjected to advertising that goes to great and very skillful lengths to drive these messages home to us.

Getting Practical

The following is an illustration from a sermon I have preached. I offer it knowing full well that others could provide examples that would better suit their situation.

You might consider the following questions as you read my comments: What do you normally think of when you hear the word stewardship? How do you feel about the particular definition of stewardship proposed in this sermon? What would it mean for you, in your own life, if you were to embrace a life of stewardship as proposed here? Would you agree that a life of intentional stewardship is not simply a one-time effort, but an ongoing journey?

In this example, I began with one of the three appointed lections for the day (Lent 2, Year C, Philippians 3:17—4:1). I first appealed to my listeners' childhood memories, and then offered a different translation of the text (J. B. Philips). I made a few brief comments to situate the text historically. Then I focused on two phrases that jumped out at me as I read the passage: "their god is their appetite" and "this world is the limit of their horizon." This presentation of scripture provided the first part of the foundation that I mentioned earlier, that is, God's dream.

Then I introduced the second part of the foundation. I asked some questions that might link this passage with our contemporary world situation: Who or what are our gods? What kinds of messages does the world give me? How is our society guided today? And I responded by suggesting, "The world society tells me that I can be happy, safe, and secure, that I can find peace and fulfilment, by acquiring, by having more and more and more, by satisfying my own hunger and thirst, my own gods."

Having given some examples from the world at large, the macro version, I then moved the focus a little more sharply on to the life of my listeners. In other words, I tried to answer the question, What does this have to do with me? "There's another God that lies beneath all these gods, another force that asks for our undivided attention. And this is the God who created the world, who gave his life so that others might live."

Having built both sides of the foundation, I then tried to establish a link between them and the listener. "Does this have any implications for my own life? What kind of a response can I make, as a person of faith who is trying to live as a disciple of Christ, and a steward of God? What does this mean for us? As followers of Jesus, we have made a decision to follow the path that Jesus walked, a path that for him led to giving much more than most of us will ever be asked to give."

Moving to my conclusion, I offered some concrete examples of what life might look like if people were to make a decision to work with God in making God's dream for them and for the world come closer to being realized. "What would this mean? For some, it might mean trying to make do with less of the material things we so often think we *need*, when in actual fact we just simply *want* them.

"For others, it might mean being intentionally more aware that all that we do have—material things, or talents and skills—have been given to us by a loving God, whose very nature is to give and give and keep on giving. For others still, it might mean giving our talents and skills, giving material things, giving money, as a way of responding to the generosity of God in our lives."

Wrapping It Up

Many years ago, I remember a friend saying to me that he believed everyone has one good sermon in them. He went on to explain that what preachers do is essentially to repeat the same thing over and over again, using different styles and techniques, in an effort to get the basic message across.

There is a great deal of truth in what my friend said. Those of us who have made an intentional commitment to live out our baptismal covenant are well aware that the Story is unchanging. How we get the story across, so as to make it attractive to others, is our challenge. How do you and I take care of God's word, which reflects God's dream? That's stewardship! How do you and I assist in making the dream come true? That's stewardship! How do we spread the word about the Word? That's stewardship!

This challenge is given to everyone, not just those called to a ministry of preaching. May you continue to become more and more aware how your words and actions reflect the kind of a steward you are, and may God continue to bless you in your stewardship journey.

Talking about Stewardship to Children and Youth

When my daughters were young, I came across a secular parenting series on audiotape that was highly influential in giving me a blueprint for raising children. Since I knew nothing about kids, I figured that, if I were going to mess up their lives, I should have a recipe from an expert.

One of the ideas presented in the tape was a plan to help children learn how to manage money. The author suggested that children be given an allowance. Here is how it worked. Give a young child allowance each week. Tell them they can choose how they use the money but that they must do three things each week: spend some of the money on themselves, save some money, and give some money to charity. Each week when the time comes for their allowance payout, the child explains how they deployed the money the previous week in order to receive the next week's allowance. Did they spend, save, and give away, and how much in each category?

This secular parenting trainer had a simple solution to the teaching of stewardship. Implicit in her methodology was an understanding of the need to think beyond ourselves to the needs of others, and the need to manage our resources wisely by saving. Furthermore, her method is theologically sound and holistic because it reinforces the joy of having money and spending it on ourselves in celebration of the abundance of God.

I have often reflected back on this simple method for instructing

From Scarcity to Abundance

children and thought to myself that this little audiotape does a much better job of teaching the essence of stewardship to kids than we do in many of our Anglican parishes.

As a parent, I didn't rely on this methodology alone. I also tried to model stewardship by taking shots at materialism when it was overtly displayed in television programs I was watching with my children. I challenged them to dissect the values that the mass media present. I talked about giving to charity; I gave to canvassers at the door just so my children would see me thinking of others and take away the lesson that it is important for them to do likewise.

We got the girls heavily involved in a Christmas gift hamper project because young children implicitly understand the joy of Christmas. The gift hamper programs that are run in many parishes provide a wonderful teachable moment to explain, in language kids understand, that we must care for the needy. I took my children to deliver hampers. As we drove away afterward, I would ponder out loud what could be done for those people year round and ask my daughters for ideas.

I became convinced that teaching children about stewardship begins at home. Nothing that we do in the parish to educate children about stewardship will be sustainable if parents are not modeling the life of stewardship and intentionally finding teachable moments to instruct their children on stewardship fundamentals. So, for me, the question becomes: How can we, as parish stewardship ministers, support parents in this task?

Here's a suggestion. As part of a Lenten study, you might hold an adult forum on early memories of money. Adults often find this experience very illuminating and even surprising. End the session with the question, What memories of money do you want your children to have? Encourage sharing, as I have done above, about how parents in the congregation are modeling stewardship fundamentals to their children.

Unfortunately, in many parishes, the stewardship journeys of children are far down on the priority list, or just not on the radar at all. I believe it is essential that we address the stewardship issue with children.

I often talk to kids about stewardship on a Sunday morning as I guest preach around the diocese. I would not, however, consider stewardship education to children one of my strengths. In my research for this chapter I found a quality web site that, I believe, will be extremely helpful if you wish to address the opportunity to educate children and youth about stewardship. In my view, the best source of ideas for teaching stewardship to children and youth is the Roman Catholic Archdiocese of St. Louis web site. I have borrowed ideas heavily and unabashedly from that web site with the graceful permission of Sue Erschen, Director of Stewardship Education of the Archdiocese of St. Louis. The web site can be found at <http://www.archstl.org/stewardship/whatis/children.html>.

Here are just a few reasons, summarized from that web site, why stewardship education to children and youth is so vital.

1. Unfortunately, in today's mass-media world, children are bombarded with materialistic messages that often lead to a sense of entitlement, and to frustration and dissatisfaction with life. Intentional efforts at stewardship teaching encourage an attitude of gratitude. We can counteract the influence of mass media by teaching children the difference between needs and wants.

2. Experts tell us that children usually form their attitudes about sharing sometime between the ages of six to ten. They will either develop an entitlement attitude: *"I don't have enough."* Or a stewardship attitude: *"I have been blessed."* (Shades of earlier discussion in this manual about the adult journey from scarcity to abundance.)

3. The advertisements that children hear in the commercial world often carry the underlying subtle message that you are not good

enough the way you are and, therefore, you need to acquire this or that product to make you acceptable. In church and at home kids need to hear a different message. They need to hear that God declares each of his children "the beloved"— good enough to inherit an overflowing measure of his love, grace, and mercy. They need to hear that God has already blessed them with all the gifts and talents that they will need. In fact, God has given them an abundance of good things, and they have enough to share.

Children can learn that stewardship is a way of life, but they need to see their parents and other influential adults modeling this.

Children can afford to be good stewards of treasure. Statistics on affluence in America reveal that the average North American child today under the age of thirteen has $230 a year in completely disposable income. This is more money than over 500 million heads of households throughout the world have to spend on food, clothing, and shelter for their families. There is nothing like a little perspective!

From the Archdiocese of St. Louis, here are a few practical ideas for teaching children about stewardship.

Make sure there is an opportunity for children to give an offering each week

It sounds obvious, but an astonishing number of congregations have never thought about this. The children's offering can come during Sunday school, children's church, or the morning worship, but it should be an event, part of the liturgy. Perhaps they will be the only group making an offering, as the adults may not be passing a collection plate. This will help make the kids feel special.

Use envelopes for children

Your parish can provide envelopes for the young people in the parish. Here are some suggestions for successfully using children's envelopes.

- Invite children to use the envelopes not only to give a small gift of treasure but also to share gifts of talent (pictures they have drawn for God, poems or prayers they have written, etc.) or pledges of time (promises to help a neighbour or parent with a chore, for example).

- Invite the children to actually come forward to the altar to place their envelopes in a basket at the foot of the altar or in a basket that the celebrant is holding. This makes children feel very special, especially when the rector personally thanks each one for his or her gift. It also is a powerful witness to the adults in the pews.

- Let the children vote on where their offertory gifts will be donated—maybe to local missions, to homeless children, to sick children, to immigrant children, to expectant mothers in need, or for a special project that the church school has adopted.

- Mail the envelopes home to the children rather than distributing them in classes. This assures that they do make it home, and that parents are aware of the fact that the child has the envelopes. Plus, kids love to receive mail, and the fact that the envelopes have been mailed makes them seem more important to children.

- Mail a letter to parents, explaining the reasons behind the program and asking for their support.

- Give an accounting of the children's collection, including the number of pictures and good deeds, in the weekly bulletin.

- Ask children in the Sunday school to create their own offertory envelope from a plain white envelope, and use that for a special one-time offertory gift.

Honor every gift

Record children's offerings and give them regular statements along with adults, regardless of the amount they contribute. If the cost

---

From Scarcity to Abundance

of keeping the records and generating the statements exceeds the amount of the contribution, so what? This is an investment in formation and is well worth the cost.

Other creative ideas

- Ask children to make stewardship posters that can be displayed in the church lobby, parish centre, and school building.

- Have your confirmation candidates create a stewardship newsletter as a class project. Childen can be assigned to interview parishioners involved in different stewardship activities in the parish. The children then write short articles about all the gifts of time and talent being given by parishioners. This newsletter can be copied and distributed to all parishioners.

- Turn children into talent scouts, having them interview one another in search of talents.

- Have the youth of the parish sponsor a specific local outreach project to expand their horizons. The Primate's World Relief and Development Fund has an excellent resource called "Side by Side," which increases awareness in youth about the world beyond Canada and lays out a program for a weekend of fund-raising and awareness-building activities.

- Run an actual stewardship campaign with the children. Provide time for self-examination about their giving of time and talents to others. Invite them to fill out a pledge card showing intent for what they would like to give to the church or other charity. Present the pledge cards in church so that the children are gifting the parish by modelling proper stewardship to adults.

One of the keys to educating children is to inculcate a sense of thanksgiving in all children. All things come from God. Help children to see that they are incredibly blessed. Get them to write about their blessings or draw pictures. Teach them to write prayers of thanksgiving or thank-you letters to God, telling him how the child will use the gifts God has given them.

Encourage parents to be creative

Stewardship education begins at home. We can encourage parents to be creative by presenting inspiring good ideas and trusting them to build upon them. Here's a story I found on the Episcopal Diocese of New York web site (http://www.dioceseny.org), with one idea inspired by a novel way to utilize a child's birthday party as a teachable moment for kids.

> My youngest daughter was recently invited to a tenth birthday party for a classmate. Nothing unusual about that. However, there was one very unique request. The guests were asked to bring food for the local food pantry instead of a gift. Since all three classes of the fourth grade were invited and most children brought a full bag, a lot of food was collected.
>
> This was a great lesson for the children, but it was an even better lesson for their parents. I'm sure many were impressed and some even inspired by this example. It is this kind of lesson that will teach people a lot more than any Sunday school lesson or sermon. [They might think:] Why don't we try something different like this story? By the way, most of the guests also brought a present for their friend.

Show children how stewardship has built their church

Children are interested in the parish church and how it got there. Here are two great ideas, again from the St. Louis Archdiocese:

- Tour parish facilities looking for signs of stewardship.
- Have older children research the "saints" of the parish and discuss the ways they were good stewards.

From Scarcity to Abundance

Questions for Consideration

1. What are we doing now to teach children and youth in our parish about stewardship in their lives?

2. Who are the people we should be pulling together to brainstorm a plan of action to promote stewardship education among our youth and children?

3. What are reasonable goals for the first year? Second year? Beyond that?

PART TWO

PARISH STEWARDSHIP: PRACTICAL AND LOGISTICAL TOOLS AND TECHNIQUES

6

The Annual Financial Stewardship Program

Sadly, in many congregations in the Canadian Anglican Church, the "annual" financial stewardship program takes place in a strategically suspect mode each autumn.

Does this sound like your parish? As the scene unfolds we normally find the rector returning from summer vacation and the wardens approaching him or her in a panic because donations have fallen off over the summer and the parish's bank line of credit is sagging under the weight of the perceived "crisis." The operating budget is not being met, and an emergency meeting is called. It's usually a very stress-filled and emotionally charged meeting.

Typically, the members of the corporation get together, review the finances, share their anxiety, and stew over what often seems like an ongoing battle that can never be won. At some point they agree. Though unsaid, the emotions are usually something along the lines of, "We feel anxious and worried. Let's make *everyone* anxious!" So bulletin messages decrying the sorry state of finances are prepared. Parish council or vestry deliberates. Someone stands up during announcement time in worship, and the anxiety is successfully spread to all.

I fear that the net impact of this common modus operandi is more destructive long-term than it is helpful in the short-term solicitation of funds to balance the operating budget. We are basically sending a negative signal with this approach to stewardship. The signal perpetuated by this activity is that the parish is in peril.

People are made to feel as though they are part of a losing enterprise, when in fact our parishes are almost always vital fixtures in the local community. Furthermore, the emphasis of this approach is on the parish's need rather than people's need to give.

One must ask why we continually find ourselves in these predicaments. It is my experience that Anglicans are very generous people. Just look at the many successful appeals to repair the roof, replace the organ, fund the refugee family, and respond to building fund campaigns. Why, then, don't Anglicans get excited about supporting parish-operating budgets?

The next two chapters are an attempt to respond to this question. In this chapter I will look at the principle of self-examination. In many ways, the logistics of parish financial stewardship efforts are all about promoting prayerful self-examination. There are many tools and techniques available to facilitate this process.

There are also several alternative programs available as "recipes" for an annual financial stewardship program. They all have positive and negative aspects. Some promote tithing, some pledging, and some proportionate giving. Recipes such as the S.T.A.R. program from the United States are purported by many Canadians to have limited use in the Canadian context. Our Lutheran cousins have a body of experience that we can tap into. The Evangelical Lutheran Church in America office in Chicago has prepared an extensive catalogue of annual financial stewardship program resources.

In the Diocese of Niagara we began a program in 1996 that our diocesan stewardship committee still strongly recommends. It is called *A Plan for Stewardship Education and Development through the Year*. The program is grounded in years of stewardship ministry by the Reverend David Gordon, who, before retirement, was doing stewardship ministry in the Episcopal Diocese of New York. I highly recommend the program; it is very practical and provides *pro forma* examples of all the documents needed to execute an annual program. The handbook detailing the program and all its elements is available from the Anglican Book Centre, written by David Gordon, with contributions by the Venerable Dr. Rick Jones of Niagara Diocese, and sells for $16.95.

The accumulated wisdom of stewardship practitioners stresses the important of putting a program in place in your parish and sticking with it year after year. This can get tedious for the stewardship team. The results are not tedious for the parish. If people become bored with the stewardship program being used, by all means change it. A new program can introduce a breath of fresh air. But the overriding principle requires that certain essential elements remain in place to encourage self-examination annually.

Elements of a Quality Invitation

These elements include

1. an explanation of the ministry of the parish;
2. individual examination of proportionate-giving habits;
3. invitations to invest in ministry at gradually increasing levels of commitment;
4. a formal pledging mechanism (nowadays, this is most often a debit program);
5. a tool to capture commitment of time and/or talent; and
6. ongoing communications about the ministry of the parish and ways to get involved.

Every few years, the use of a tool to aid in the discernment of spiritual gifts would be most appropriate. Bill Easum and many others have published useful guides to discerning spiritual gifts. One of the best I have discovered is called *The Three Colors of Ministry,* written by Christian Schwartz and Brigitte Berief-Schwartz, and published by the Natural Church Development Institute. It's available through the NCD web site at <http://www.ncd-international. org/BooksMinistry.html>.

Let's look at the six items on this list individually.

1. An Explanation of the Ministry of the Parish

Today's sophisticated donors want to know that their money is being spent wisely and will have a long life. Charities such as hospitals, universities, the Salvation Army, Cancer Society, and the United Way all put a good deal of effort into explaining the nature, scope, and impact of their work to their donor base. The local parish must do the same in an environment where competition for the philanthropic dollar is fierce. The next chapter on narrative budgeting takes a deeper look at how we tell our parish's story.

There is a maxim in stewardship. I was once told to never forget that our members don't give *to* the church; they give *through* the church to touch the lives of other people. We need to be auditing all stewardship communication through the filter of this insight.

Ask yourself whether the communication piece being utilized is effectively illustrating how donors' money is being deployed to impact the lives of others. When we do this well, experience shows that people will find much to feel passionate about and will open their hearts and their check-books.

2. Individual Examination of Proportionate-Giving Habits

David Gordon, in discussing proportionate giving, writes:

> "Proportionate giving" means that shares of our personal resources of time and talents and treasure are being devoted to the Lord's work on a regular schedule. It is a commitment

made in response to the love which God has shown for us through His Son, Jesus Christ, as well as in events of daily life. It is an offering of "ourselves, our souls and bodies."

Tithing is a standard by which we measure our offerings. All that we are and all that we have has come from God and still belongs to God and is to be used for God's glory. Within that context, the biblical tithe (10 percent) becomes a minimum goal in deciding what portion of our resources will be given [Gordon, 1998, 33].

I believe that the "genius" of the year-round financial steward-ship education program used in Niagara Diocese is the use of the proportionate-giving worksheet (see below and appendix 3). This worksheet, developed by David Gordon and modified later by his son John, is completed in the privacy of one's home, and no one ever sees it but the donor. Gordon thinks of proportionate giving as making "a personal policy decision"—a decision to include the Lord's work in the family budget.

It is an invitation. It invites the donor to examine current giving levels, and consider giving levels for the following year. Ideally, it is distributed with the parish's Narrative Budget document, giving context to the donor's reflections.

The worksheet is segmented into two parts as you can see below.

Part 1—Current Giving

	Example	Your Figures
A. Current Income	$30,000	$_____
B. Current Annual Donation	$ 600	$_____
C. Current Percentage Level (Divide line B by line A)	2%	_____%

It really doesn't matter whether the donor uses gross or net income figures in reflecting on these calculations. The point is to invite donors to think about their personal financial stewardship from this perspective.

The second part of the worksheet looks like this:

Part 2—Next Year's Commitment

A financial commitment for the upcoming year might be based on one of the following options:

A. Tithing

	Example	*Your Figures*
1. Expected Income	$30,000	$_____
2. The Biblical Tithe	10%	_____ 10%
3. New Commitment	$ 3,000	$_____
(Multiply line 1 by line 2)		

B. Increasing the Present Level by 1%

	Example	*Your Figures*
1. Expected Income	$30,000	$_____
2. Current Percentage plus 1%	3%	_____%
3. New Commitment	$ 900	$_____

C. Adopting the Parish Goal

	Example	*Your Figures*
1. Expected Income	$30,000	$_____
2. Parish Minimum Percentage Goal	2.5%	_____%
3. New Commitment	$ 750	$_____

Adapted from John D. Gordon, Christ Church, Seattle, WA.

When a canvasser from the Heart and Stroke Foundation or Cancer Society comes to my door, I always ask them how my neighbours are responding. They tell me that people are giving $10 or $20 and, unwittingly, they are giving me a context to make my decision on how much to give.

The proportionate-giving worksheet gives context. I think we fail to realize that many people are unsure of how much to give. The proportionate-giving worksheet holds up the biblical tithe and the parish minimum percentage goal as context. It should not, however, be used in isolation. It is a tool that must be accompanied by teaching about moving, over time, toward the tithe. This teaching can be done in many ways, and should always be incorporated into an accompanying cover letter to the donor.

The proportionate-giving worksheet should not be underestimated. Many people find it facilitates an "aha" moment for them as they view their financial stewardship in a new way. The worksheet in appendix 3 of this primer also outlines a calculation for the commitment of time and talent.

3. An Invitation to Invest in Ministry at Gradually Increasing Levels of Commitment

By utilizing tools such as the proportionate-giving worksheet annually, we attempt to move donors toward an increasing commitment to the ministry of their parish by holding up the biblical tithe as an ideal. Our task is to issue a *quality* invitation. What would this be like? The short answer is that it contains all the components discussed in this chapter. A quality invitation promotes prayerful self-examination, explains how money and talent will be used to impact lives, and includes a formal mechanism to "close the deal."

4. A Formal Pledging Mechanism

One of the most difficult challenges facing parish stewardship ministry is encouraging members to make a *formal* financial commitment to the ministry of the parish. In trying to affect this, many run up against a culture where pledging has not been part of the status quo. Unfortunately, many Anglicans bristle at the thought of filling out a pledge card to their parish. Moving toward pledging in this type of parish is not for the squeamish. I know of one parish that encouraged people to pledge and then offered the pledge cards on the altar during worship, only to burn them, thus fulfilling a promise to the parish not to open the envelopes containing the pledge cards. That parish saw the necessity for pledging, convinced donors to complete the cards, but couldn't take the next step. I suspect that by bailing out on the pledge system, although with good intentions, they actually perpetuated the existing culture.

Let's look at the reasons why people might be reticent to fill out a pledge card for their parish's annual operating budget.

1. In some parishes pledging may be a new concept. Many parishes have no historical tradition of pledging. Reasons vary for this void. In some places a strong parishioner has been against pledging and has intimidated the leadership. In other places local employment levels have fluctuated widely, and people have consequently been nervous about pledging. In some parishes the clergy have not championed this practice, making it hard to implement.

2. Individual reasons for being unwilling to embrace pledging are equally diverse. For some people, there is indignation that a charity is seen as "demanding" a commitment from them. Education is necessary here. These people need to learn that it costs money to do ministry. They can be reminded that almost all organizations would be labeled irresponsible if they didn't undertake forward planning. By asking for their pledged commitment, the local parish is being responsible in its forward planning process.

3. Other reasons often articulated for reluctance to pledge stem

from concerns about instability of donors' income and/or expenses. Donors sincerely don't want to make a financial commitment if they have fears or insecurity around their ability to fulfil that commitment. I have found it helpful to reassure donors that they are under no obligation to fulfil their pledge should their financial circumstances suffer dramatic reversals. This issue can be especially relevant to the very elderly, who have a strong sense of commitment and duty, but don't know how long they will inhabit this planet.

It helps to explain to people who are reluctant to pledge that a pledge is merely a statement of intent, designed to help parish leadership plan the ministry of the parish for the coming year. If resistance is particularly strong, you don't need to call it a pledge card. Call it a "commitment card" or better still, a "statement of intent card." You can also make the pledge-response mechanism more useful and multi-faceted by incorporating an option for the commitment of time and talent.

Sometimes the barrier to pledging is situated squarely in the lap of leadership. While running a stewardship workshop recently at a diocese in the Maritimes, I was told that virtually no one in the diocese pledged. In this diocese, there are genuine issues around job stability in rural areas. Maybe in your diocese there needs to be some intentional teaching about pledging at the diocesan level—the diocesan newspaper or articles on the diocesan web site might be a place to start. In parishes where pledging is just not part of the culture, there is a fear of donor revolt if pledging is initiated. Look honestly at your situation. Is the main stumbling block the resistance of the donor base or your fear of addressing the pledging void?

Having said all this, one cannot overestimate the importance of a pledging mechanism in the annual stewardship financial campaign. A pledge card is the final step in an intentional process of self-examination. It is a declaration of intent that puts in place a commitment that has developed out of all the rest of the stewardship educational efforts.

If you are in a parish that has not pledged, you need to be realistic in your expectations. Initiating pledging will meet some resistance and will certainly not achieve 100% participation. But if you stick with it, participation will build and pledging can become the norm. Instituting pledging provides many teachable moments for the stewardship team. It can be used to help reinforce the reality that doing ministry costs money, and that the gospel good news of God's abundant care requires a response. (A sample of a pledge card for an annual commitment drive can be found in appendix 5 of this handbook.)

PAP Programs—a Better Way to Pledge

If pledging is just not going to happen, concentrate your efforts on implementing pre-authorized monthly offerings via debit. A pre-authorized payment (PAP) program is better than a pledge. It has all the elements of a pledge and a concrete mechanism to make the actual gift a reality. It is also much more familiar to most donors as they already pay many bills that way.

Ultimately, putting your efforts into increasing the number of parishioners on PAP automatic debt may be a much better use of your time than fighting the uphill battle of instituting pledging from scratch. In places where there is no culture of pledging this is almost certainly a much more productive strategy.

If pledging is so foreign and counter-cultural to your parish that implementing is nearly impossible, look at the case study in chapter 10 and try the innovative idea our case parish came up with.

A Word about Newcomers

There is a difference of opinion on when to invite newcomers to participate in parish life. Most of the literature seems to indicate that it takes eighteen months to integrate a newcomer into a parish.

We need to be sensitive to this reality. It takes people time to feel that they are part of a faith community. During the early months, when people are testing out a parish, it is probably not a good idea to push pledging on them. However, newcomer material should address expectations of membership in your parish.

One highly successful parish I know of states in its hospitality material that members are expected to give at least 2% of income to the parish and to be working toward the biblical tithe over time. We do know that stewardship education *must* start right away with the unchurched or later attempts at stewardship awareness will be of limited success. Laying out expectations to new members is a good way to start that teaching.

5. A Tool to Capture Commitment of Time and Talent

The stewardship committee can help people see the commitment of their time and talent as an outward sign of where they are in their spiritual journey. Talk of financial stewardship may create an impression that stewardship is solely about money. This is a real danger because money is often our focus. We do our congregations a disservice if we ignore the full scope of Christian stewardship. Many congregations have developed a mechanism to encourage self-examination of the deployment of time and talent.

The proportionate-giving worksheet example in appendix 3 of this book shows a calculation for the pledging of time. The most practical vehicle seems to be an 8-1/2 X 11 inches two-sided sheet attached to financial pledge cards. This sheet lists all the ministries in a parish and asks people to check the ministries they would like to get involved with in the coming year. It also invites them to pledge 10% of their free time. An added benefit of this tool is that it gives volunteers the opportunity to consider new ministries and to renew themselves by doing different ministry within the parish. One caveat, however: If you ask people to indicate ministries they would like to get involved in, you must follow up.

I remember standing up in a parish meeting and asking for volunteers to cut the cemetery lawn. One gentleman graciously pointed out that his time and talent card had indicated that he would help with lawn cutting, but he had never been called. This example points out the need in many parishes for a volunteer coordinator. *Remember when doing a mailing to parish households to include one pledge form for time and talent for each member of the household over the age of ten. Even younger children need to be encouraged to be good stewards of their time and talent.* Write each member's name on the top of each time and talent pledge form.

The other benefit of encouraging the commitment of time and talent is that it provides an opportunity for people to explore and discover their spiritual gifts. This is an integral component of any stewardship ministry in a parish.

Calculating the impact of the time parishioners put into various parish ministries is a real eye-opener in many places. If you add up the time that goes into a Sunday service, you may be surprised. For example, ten choir members practicing two hours on Thursday and attending liturgy two hours on Sunday makes forty hours a week of volunteer time. In addition, altar guild members, servers, greeters, money counters, chalice bearers, readers, and intercessors give countless hours to the church. It all adds up.

In some parishes eighty to a hundred hours go into worship on a Sunday. Multiply that by fifty-two weeks, and then consider all the Bible study, pastoral care, youth ministry, church school, bookkeeping, outreach, fellowship, and other volunteer time, and you will see that even a medium size parish can use over 10,000 hours a year of volunteer time. And many churches use much more. Sharing this kind of calculation can create a positive change in how a parish views itself and its place in the community. Regardless of where people are financially, *every* member of the parish is capable of tithing their time.

It is a very real and tangible truth of the faith journey that people find fulfilment and joy in the utilization of their spiritual gifts.

I typed the preceeding sentence in its own paragraph and italicized it so that it would be isolated and you could look back and re-read and digest it. This point is central to the role of the leader in the stewardship ministry of the local parish. By encouraging and facilitating the use of spiritual gifts we are gifting the parish and its membership.

6. Ongoing Communication about the Ministry of the Parish

One must not underestimate the importance of regular and informative communication with the congregation about the ministry of the parish and ways to get involved. Many parishes hold an annual ministry fair after Sunday services in September and invite each of the ministries of the parish to present volunteer opportunities in booths in parish halls. Ideas abound.

I know of churches where a member of a parish group (for example, altar guild or choir) is invited to stand up and talk about that group and its ministry during announcement time. Each week a representative from a different group is asked to speak. The parish newsletter is a wonderful vehicle to talk about the parish and the impact it is making internally and on the local or wider community. Perhaps you are already doing many of these things in your parish. The key is to continue to communicate throughout the year while emphasizing how the deployment of time, talent, and treasure is making an impact in people's lives.

The narrative budgeting process also provides many opportunities to share the sacred corporate story of the parish and its ministry. This is where we turn our attention next.

Questions for Reflection

1. What are your personal feelings and experience about pledging to the church?

2. Does your parish have a history of pledging? Does it have a history of in-home face-to-face visitation to discuss commitment to the ministry of the parish? What are the obstacles to pledging and visitation in your parish?

3. How are newcomers encouraged and invited to support the ministry of the church?

4. When was the last time your parish did education around discernment of spiritual gifts? Does your parish have a way to help its members discover and develop their spiritual gifts?

5. In what ways does your parish challenge individual members to use their talents/gifts to further the ministry of the parish?

6. Reflect on how you have found fulfilment in using your spiritual gifts in a volunteer capacity or in the workplace.

7

Narrative Budgeting: Our Corporate Sacred Story

Narrative budgeting has a *critical* role to play in any comprehensive parish stewardship program. Given what we know about donor dynamics and motivation, there are compelling reasons to distribute a Narrative Budget every year in your parish.

In the last chapter I asked why Anglicans don't support annual operating budgets with the enthusiasm they bring to other church projects. Basic philanthropic theory indicates that people want their money to have an impact. Narrative budgeting is the best tool I have found to demonstrate to donors how their money and time are filtering *through* the church to touch the lives of people in need.

Every week we come together around The Story—the Good News we find in the revelation of Jesus Christ. It is a story that is life-defining and transforming for each one of us. Earlier in this manual we reflected also on our personal sacred stewardship story. I have argued that, as individuals, we all have a sacred story about God's loving care in our lives and about our response to God's abundance. Each faith community also has a sacred story about how the community has responded in thanksgiving to God's call to be the church in the place where it is planted.

The basic assumption behind narrative budgeting is that donors are reluctant to give money to operating budgets when they do not have a clear indication of how their donation is making an impact in people's lives through the ministry of the parish. The traditional line-item budget, which most parishes work from throughout the year and present to donors at annual meetings, is a good accounting and planning tool but, I would submit, a terrible marketing tool to motivate donor investment in ministry.

Think of your own motivation to give. Are you inspired by the fact that your donation is funding the postage meter and photocopier? Do you get all tingly inside knowing your donation will help pay for heat and electricity? If you do, you are a rare donor and you may just need to get a life! Most donors can't get excited about giving to administration and fixed overhead expenses. Sure, they know these expenses are a necessary component of running a parish, but they certainly don't want to think about them.

Step 1—Making a Start

Narrative budgeting looks first at the various ministries of the parish and then assigns all anticipated expenses to one of six key areas of ministry. In most parishes it is relatively easy to designate several areas and then begin to allocate expenses against these areas. Let me explain by giving an example.

Imagine that the leaders in the parish of St. Paul's sit down and talk about their ministry to each other and the wider community. After some discussion they agree on the following six areas of ministry that encompass what parish life is all about:

- worship;
- pastoral care;
- outreach;
- Christian education and formation;
- evangelism and hospitality;
- fellowship and inreach.

Any parish could decide to use this template of six categories in the first year of implementing narrative budgeting in the parish. However, every parish is unique, and these categories may not be exactly appropriate for your parish. You may decide, for example, that you need a separate category for youth and children's ministry because that may be a huge component of your parish's self-understanding. In the above example, I would include youth and children's ministry under Christian education and formation.

Notice that there is no category titled administration. That would be counter to the very essence of narrative budgeting. We want to reframe the way people think. We want them to clearly understand their faith community as a non-secular institution that looks at the world and its mission with non-secular glasses. Notice, too, that there are only six categories. Experience has shown that six categories make an ideal number to help people understand the ministry of the parish.

After the six categories have been determined, a small group—two or three parish leaders and the rector—sits down and talks about allocating all the line items in the operating budget to each of the six categories of ministry. Some items are easy to allocate. The choir director's salary fits perfectly in the worship category, as do the costs of candles, hymn books, communion wafers, wine, Sunday bulletin photocopies, and miscellaneous altar guild expenses. The cost of offertory envelopes fits into Christian education and formation, as stewardship education is an element of our overall Christian formation.

Narrative budgeting is an art, not a science. Many areas of work are not clearly delineated. You will need to ask your paid staff to diarize their activities for a month. At the end of a month, they should have a sense of how they allocate their time against the six categories. If the rector spends 20% of her time in pastoral care, allocate 20% of her salary and benefits against the pastoral care category. The same principle applies with the parish secretary, and other staff. I suggest to parishes that, once the rector has determined his or her time allocation among the six categories, leadership then has a blueprint to follow for the allocation of other overhead expenses such as heat, hydro, phone, and rectory expenses.

If you are nervous about the accuracy of this allocation process, I would like to give you permission to lighten up. Make your best guesses based on a deliberate review of time allocation, but don't burden yourself with over-worry about accuracy. Be as correct as you can, but understand this fundamental insight—the Narrative Budget is a snapshot of parish activity, and a marketing and education tool. Its purpose is to help donors appreciate and become more aware of how their money is ultimately affecting people's lives and making an impact. It is *not* an accounting tool.

You will feel more comfortable each year that you undertake this process. In the early years you are attempting in good faith to give people a new, non-secular way of thinking about the ministry of their parish. We are *not* a business. But from business models we learn that we must market our ministry to donors because, in effect, we are asking them to invest in us. But we do it our way, faithful to the knowledge that we are people of the story.

Ultimately, regardless of the actual percentage amount, we want donors to take away something like this:

20¢ of every dollar I give is going to pastoral care;
32¢ of every dollar I give is going to outreach;
10¢ of every dollar I give is going to evangelism and hospitality;
23¢ of every dollar I give is going to worship;
7¢ of every dollar I give is going to fellowship and inreach;
8¢ of every dollar I give is going to Christian education and formation.

Therefore, the money I give is making an impact in very concrete ways.

Jim Newman, Director of Stewardship with the Diocese of Niagara, has developed software that is available, and downloadable, from the Niagara diocesan web site, to help you create your parish's Narrative Budget. That software includes Excel spreadsheet templates for inputting line-item amounts into the different categories, and it generates pie charts for looking at each of the six categories, or all six together. The pie charts express spending by percentage and illustrate different ministry categories via color-coding. That is the first stage to putting together your parish's Narrative Budget. The web site address to download these templates is <http://www.niagara. anglican.ca/synodsteward.htm>.

Step 2—Telling the Story

Once you have allocated all your expenses via each of the six categories unique to your parish, you need to tell the story. In presenting a Narrative Budget to the congregation, you want to tell the story of each of the six categories.

In the outreach category, for example, you have an opportunity to do parish education that highlights all the outreach ministries. For each of the six categories you could prepare a parish mailing or Sunday morning handout telling the story. In my example parish, the outreach story is layered and might look something like this:

Outreach ministries include

- program to drive seniors to doctors' appointments and run other errands;

- public school breakfast program;

- support of local ecumenical food bank;

- Friday night youth drop-in center;

- Christmas hamper program for families in crisis;

- job-hunting skills workshops;

- support program for single working moms with small children;

- annual donations to the Primate's World Relief and Development Fund;

- youth trip to Honduras to help build a school;

- prison ministry Sunday afternoons;

- mission assessment to the diocese and national church.

In your narrative you will need to explain the details of each of these ministries. You can outline each program and help people to understand how it works. Often, when we are heavily involved in the ministry of a parish, we make the mistake of assuming that others are as knowledgeable as we are about what the parish is doing in the community. A common response from parishioners is that they were unaware that the parish was doing so much in the individual categories of ministry.

Peeling Back the Onion

Then you will need to peel back the onion even more. After first telling the overall story of the specific ministry, you then proceed to make it much more personal. Tell the story of specific individuals touched by the ministry. For instance:

> Jimmy is an inmate at the local medium-security correctional institute. He has two estranged sons, and they live 1,500 miles away in Bangor, Maine. He has no other family. Every other Sunday, four volunteers from the parish attend the facility and put on a worship service. Before and after the service they sit and talk with the inmates, bring them books and magazines, the occasional chocolate bar and smokes.
>
> Jimmy loves cars and has fond memories of working on an old roadster with his uncle when he was a teenager. The parish outreach fund paid for a birthday gift of a year's subscription to *Car and Driver* magazine for him. Jimmy has no financial

resources and the parish outreach fund also deposits $10 a month in Jimmy's canteen account at the prison.

In tears last Christmas, Jimmy told a volunteer from the parish that we were the only visitors he'd had in the past four years. Jesus reminds us that whenever we visit the prisoner it is His face we encounter.

Here is another example:

Gladys lives alone in a small one-bedroom apartment in the same block as the church. She is eighty-four now and no longer able to drive. She really can't afford a move to a retirement home, as the only local option would cost her over $2,400 a month, and she does not have the financial resources.

Four years ago a group of concerned parishioners put together a team to care for local seniors. The building where Gladys lives is close by and has many seniors in similar circumstances to Gladys. It was a natural choice when a local needs-assessment was done by the parish outreach committee.

Once a week Audrey from the parish picks Gladys up and takes her grocery shopping and to the bank. Audrey checks on Gladys by phone and makes sure she is okay. Last week she drove Gladys to her doctor's appointment and then to pick up the prescription the doctor wrote. Once a month Audrey brings Gladys to the parish hall for a seniors' luncheon. There is always a guest speaker at these luncheons and a honorarium is occasionally paid to the speaker from the outreach fund. The meal is free and paid for from the fund. Afterwards the group plays cards and then Gladys and the others are driven home.

Gladys and Audrey have become close friends. They have found the face of Jesus in each other. Gladys wrote the rector thanking him for how the parish has cared for her. In her letter she said that she doesn't know what she would do without Audrey and the nice people at St. Paul's.

As we peel back the onion, the sacred story of the parish's ministry to real people takes on a new meaning and resonates at deep levels with what we are supposed to be about as faithful Christians. Experience shows, that as Anglicans see that their money is impacting on lives, they are extremely generous. I can't help but believe that narrative budgeting creates teachable moments about the church's call in the world and deepens faith journeys of donors.

Narrative budgeting can be expanded over time to include pie charts detailing how volunteer *time* in the parish is divided among the six categories of ministry. Although it tends to be used primarily on the expense side of the budget, Niagara Diocese's software can also be used to show revenue generation. Over time, the parish can use the Narrative Budget to evaluate its mission response to the gospel. Sometimes the process will draw attention to reduced commitment to an area of ministry. It will highlight in stark relief if one of the areas of ministry such as outreach or pastoral care is trending lower in commitment percentage over time.

I want to say a word about what is, admittedly, a personal bias of mine. When allocating expenses between outreach and evangelism, I want to make sure that the difference between the two is clearly defined. Evangelism is spreading the good news of Jesus Christ, welcoming newcomers, advertising, promotion, and other congregational development expenses intended to promote growth in numbers and invite people to discover the transformative power of the gospel. This is not the classical definition of outreach. Outreach expenses promote social service and social justice for the sake of ministering to people in need, and not evangelizing them.

Step 3—Creating Awareness of the Narrative Budget

In most parishes, the Narrative Budget is presented in totality to the congregation at the annual meeting. That meeting can present an opportunity to do some education around the mission and ministry of the parish. In the first few years, the process used to develop the Narrative Budget should be explained. I would recommend taking extra time on the agenda to describe each of the six areas at length. Copies of the Narrative Budget should be available to everyone in the meeting.

Parishes are encouraged *not* to take the line-item budget to the annual meeting.

Once you have a Narrative Budget, the line-item budget becomes a backup document and should no longer be widely disseminated. This advice may be contentious and hard to hear. Your initial reaction may be that it is counter-cultural in your parish. But it is actually vital.

We are a Christian organization, and we do not look at the deployment of our financial resources the way the business world does. As stewardship ministers, we are engaged in an education process. We are trying to teach congregants to move away from a secular way of viewing our ministry. I realize that there are people in every parish who are accountant types who want to view the line-item information. We have to assure them that the background financial statements that the bank and the diocese require have been done. You can make copies of the line-item budget available through the church office. Tell parishioners that five copies of the line-item budget have been made and can be signed out of the parish office for viewing and then returned.

Please understand why this is important. Many parishes show both the narrative and line-item budgets, and undermine the good work that they are attempting through implementing narrative budgeting. The very act of widely disseminating the line-item budget sends the parish mixed messages. It says, "We want you to look at our parish ministry in two ways." But in reality, we *don't* want people to look at our ministry in two ways. We want to reframe our budgeting process and teach people to view our parish ministry solely from the perspective of the work the parish is doing to be responsive to the gospel call on our lives.

If you think this will create a harsh backlash against the rector, wardens, and stewardship team, get the parish council to vote before vestry to present in this way. Then you can tell the vestry you have the full support of the parish council in moving toward narrative budgeting and away from long, tedious discussions about line-item details. The vestry meeting then becomes a meeting about mission and ministry instead of an annual business meeting of the faith community.

You may wish to utilize the power point presentation created to introduce parish councils to narrative budgeting that is available on the Niagara diocesan web site. You have permission to use this material and can access a downloadable copy of this presentation at <http://www.niagara.anglican.ca/synodsteward.htm>.

It is very important to distribute the Narrative Budget (in booklet form) with the annual stewardship mailing that contains the proportionate-giving worksheet and pledge card or pre-authorized payment form. The Narrative Budget gives context to the calculations of the worksheet and the completion of a pledge card. Used properly and in context, the Narrative Budget increases commitment and giving levels.

In closing, I pray that you will find narrative budgeting a valuable tool in your stewardship education ministry. Through it you will tell your corporate sacred story and give people an opportunity to reflect on how they can intersect with that story and truly be partners in the parish's ministry. Make a beginning! You will find it gets easier every year and that people actually look forward to learning more of the story of the parish and its good work.

Questions for Reflection

1. What are the barriers to implementing narrative budgeting in your parish? Who will have to buy into narrative budgeting to make it happen?

2. What six categories of parish ministry would be most appropriate for your parish?

3. What are the ministries that are crucial components of your parish's self-identity?

4. Are you primarily an outreach parish? A worship and spirituality parish? An evangelism parish? A pastoral care parish? Why did you answer the way you did?

5. What are some of the sacred stories of the people touched by your parish's ministry? Over the years? This year?

8

Coping with Limited Volunteer Resources

Whose responsibility is stewardship in your parish? Can one person carry the ball without the help of others?

The simple answer is that living the principles of Christian stewardship is the responsibility of all the baptized. Practically, however, someone has to take on the responsibility of stewardship quarterback. *I have become convinced that, as the chief theologian of the parish, the rector must be that leader.* A parish where the rector is unconvinced, uninterested, or feels inadequate in matters of stewardship is in deep trouble and will lose the confidence and financial support of the people.

In football, the offensive line knows their job is to get creamed and to cream their defensive opponents. They have to have confidence in the leader that their sacrifices help achieve a greater goal. The team works when all on the offensive line trust that their quarterback is also willing to sacrifice himself for the greater goals of the team. The receivers run their routes because they know from experience that the ball will be there when they turn and look back.

What I am trying to convey with this football analogy is that people will act sacrificially if they trust that their leader is competent, has a vision, and is acting sacrificially. It is a reality in the North American Church that the people look to the rector as leader to model and promote sound biblical principles of stewardship. Without that leadership, the people will not follow. But the rector, while setting the tone and being the primary educator, must have help and should *never* have to carry the stewardship ball alone in a parish.

One of the pitfalls of writing a stewardship primer for use across the North American Church is the issue of parish size and the available volunteer resource pool. If you are a member of a large parish where you turn away stewardship volunteers, you can skip this chapter. If you are in the other 99.8% of parishes in the North American Church, you know that blanket instructions on how to run year-round stewardship education and development programs with ten keen volunteers have limited relevance to a parish lucky to have one or two involved in the ministry of stewardship.

Where you are working with limited volunteer support you must adjust your goals and objectives for year-round stewardship education. You probably don't have to adjust your goals for Planned Giving and the occasional Capital Campaign, however. Planned Giving is not labor intensive and parish Capital Campaigns, when well conceived, usually generate enough short-term enthusiasm and volunteers to be workable.

Regardless of size, every parish needs a stewardship champion to work with the public support and blessing of the rector. Here's my current wisdom on what skills and qualities that person should possess:

Job Description for a Parish Stewardship Champion

If your parish is looking for someone to champion the stewardship ministry, you might want to consider the following job description.

Position Summary

The position has two very distinct areas of responsibility.

The parish stewardship champion (use the title your parish likes for this ministry) is responsible to the rector and wardens for the planning and execution of specific strategies related to stewardship education initiatives in the parish, fund-raising campaigns, and special events, and recruiting and support of a parish Planned Giving representative.

The parish stewardship champion also works with the corporation, volunteers, and diocesan office staff (where appropriate) to develop stewardship tools as part of the annual operating budget pledge campaign.

Depending on local parish needs, involvement in fund-raising, special events, and Planned Giving may be delegated or shared beyond the parish stewardship champion.

Responsibilities

Stewardship Initiatives

1. Initiate a year-round stewardship education program to enable the parishes to achieve their stewardship goals by issuing parishioners an annual invitation that promotes self-examination. Promote and market the importance of this program to parish council, volunteers, and parishioners.

2. Familiarize yourself with the various tools and stewardship vehicles available. Where appropriate, connect with diocesan or national church stewardship consultants.

3. Set goals for the implementation of narrative budgeting and increased pre-authorized payment programs in the parish. Work with the parish treasurer and corporation to develop the Narrative Budget.

4. Preach on stewardship in the parish when appropriate at the invitation of rector and wardens. Or encourage others to preach a regular stewardship message. See chapter 4 on preaching stewardship.

Planned Giving

1. Work with the rector and corporation to identify, recruit, train, and support a Planned Giving parish representative. Include that representative as part of the parish stewardship team. (Maybe that will make two of you!)

General

Attend diocesan stewardship workshops and, where appropriate, annual stewardship training events.

Qualifications

- Good communication skills, both verbal and written.

- Demonstrated knowledge of, and a personal commitment to, Christian stewardship principles. Be a giver. If treasure is an issue, be a giver of time and talent.

- Computer literacy is helpful in order to coordinate the implementation of narrative budgeting

This simple job description gives a parish enough information to recruit a parish stewardship champion. The parish then needs to provide that champion with the resources to take on this ministry. At the very minimum this will include some administrative support and financial commitment toward the cost of regular communication with the parish.

The champion will need help in putting together narrative budgeting, and a willingness to articulate a mission that the stewardship team (champion) can use to market the parish's ministry to donors. Parish stewardship volunteers should be commissioned in front of the parish during worship, be provided space in newsletters and bulletins, and given time in parish council meetings and during announcements to undertake education to the membership at large. It is key that the parish regard the stewardship task as a ministry.

For too long, stewardship has been viewed as an unenviable task. Instead, it needs to be seen as a vibrant and vital ministry in the life of the parish.

Rewards for Parish Stewardship Volunteers

In many parishes the stewardship role is viewed as the job no one wants. It is often given to the new person on parish council, who is left to figure out a program largely without help. How unfortunate that is. The stewardship task should and can be a vibrant ministry that brings revitalization and renewal to an entire parish. It is much too important to the life of a faith community to be treated as an unpleasant task that no one wants.

We have seen that all disciples of Jesus are on a journey. From a stewardship perspective it is a journey from a spirituality of scarcity to a spirituality of abundance. What a gift and sacred trust it is to be a companion on that journey. As stewardship volunteers, we gift our congregations by helping them grow in their personal stewardship. We help them discover that they are made in the image of "the Great Giver," that they can find joy in giving and fulfilment in the use of their spiritual gifts. It is a wonderful blessing to the stewardship volunteer to be part of this process and lead fellow congregants deeper into their sacred stories and journeys.

A Five-Point Plan for Stewardship Where Volunteer Resources Are Limited

If limited volunteer resources inhibit your parish from running a full-blown annual stewardship education program, such as the one described earlier in this manual, there are still some important activities that are the bare minimum and must be done annually.

In the absence of a comprehensive program, I believe even smaller parishes can execute a modified five-step program and achieve substantial results. The key to an effective program with limited volunteer resources is a strategy that promotes prayerful self-examination and delivers a quality invitation to donors. The key to making a modified program work is to set measurable objectives.

1. The single most important thing you can do is prepare a Narrative Budget and put it in the hands of every identifiable giver on the parish rolls, each year with the fall stewardship mailing. *This goal is easy to measure. You either do it or you don't!*

2. Put the proportionate-giving worksheet in the hands of all identifiable givers, along with a covering letter inviting parishioners to a time of self-examination, using the worksheet as a tool. *Again, easy to measure. You either mail/deliver the worksheet to all donors or you don't.*

3. Put a pledge card with categories for treasure and time into the hands of all identifiable givers, every year in a mailing that follows up the proportionate-giving worksheet and narrative budgeting mailing by two weeks. (To save costs and consolidate the annual program, mail the pledge card, the proportionate-giving worksheet, the Narrative Budget, and the covering letter from parish leadership all together.)

4. Set a goal for increasing the number of families on pre-authorized payment for giving to the parish. Pre-authorized payments are automatic deductions from parishioner bank accounts authorized by the donor. If you have twenty families on pre-authorized payment, set a goal of thirty. Then forty the following year. Be relentless. Tell the parish you are not letting up on promoting this initiative until you have reached your annual goal. *Measure success versus the absolute number objective.*

5. Strategic Visiting. The purpose of strategic visiting is face-to-face communication of the sacred corporate story. The objective

is to raise awareness of the many ministries of the parish and invite people to participate with time and talent in that ministry. It is not necessary to bring up commitment of treasure during this visitation. Do what works in your local parish culture.

With limited volunteer resources you may wish to arrange your parish list into three groups. You can decide how to allocate these groups. One suggestion would be to segment it into (1) the core members, (2) those giving but not substantially, and (3) those on the perimeter of parish life. You could then choose, over time, to visit just those in one of these three segments.

Another option is to plan visits around other strategic opportunities. For example, one year you may wish to visit just newcomers; another year you may choose to visit everyone giving $100 to $300 a year with a compelling message about the need for greater support. You choose, based on the strategic opportunities you identify.

Remember, the strategic message for a visit must be customized for each group being visited. Your leadership can brainstorm what primary message is strategically sound for parishioners in each of the different groups.

Some Practical Tips for Visiting Parishioners

Ask any priest and you will discover that the two hardest ministries to recruit for are Sunday school teachers and stewardship visitors. People are intimidated by the prospect of asking someone they know for money, and they run the other way when they hear that the parish is recruiting visitors. Some faithful Anglicans have been known to temporarily subscribe to "call display" when they hear an every-member visitation is around the corner.

The key to successful visitation is training. Let's try to unpack how we can demystify the stewardship visitation and make it an enjoyable experience for both the person visiting and the person visited.

When recruiting visitors, explain first that all visitors will be trained thoroughly before being asked to undertake this task. Tell them that you are not asking them to take on a long-term ministry, but a specific short-term ministry with a beginning and ending date, all within a two- or three-month timeframe. Speak in terms of the number of visits and number of hours of commitment needed. When people see that only six or seven hours of their time is being solicited, they are more likely to be responsive to your recruitment pitch.

Set aside a specific evening or Sunday after church for training. Open in prayer and situate the planned visits within a theological framework (see chapter 4, "Taking Care of the Word: Preaching about Stewardship"). Go slowly over any materials you have developed and invite questions while allowing time for visitors to read the materials. Go over the steps of the visit. Role-play a visit with another parish leader, then break the group up and have visitors role-play being both visitor and visitee.

Have plenty of handouts. Prepare the visitor with simple, un-complicated materials to leave behind, and fact sheets with answers to questions they are liable to encounter on their visits.

As parish leaders you may determine that your visitation will include a request for a financial commitment. Many visitors are loathe to discuss money with parishioners they know and are even more reticent with strangers. Conventional church wisdom is to remind visitors that they have nothing to be apologetic about (they are asking for the church and not for themselves); that it costs money to do ministry; and that those being visited know that the visitor's job is difficult and will be very friendly toward the visitor.

All these factors, while true, do not help someone who has never asked for a gift to a charity or the church before. There is a secret insight that has helped me to go into people's living rooms and talk very intentionally about specific amounts of money. *It is much easier to discuss money when I know that the commitment I am asking for from the donor is not going to affect their standard of living in any appreciable way.* They will still go out for lunch after church, take their annual vacation, buy a new car when the old one dies, and help the grandkids with university expenses. I find it easier to invite a donor to make a financial commitment to the ministry of the parish when I can frame it in the context of the lives of people being touched by the parish's ministry.

Stewardship Visitor Checklist

The following checklist is helpful for visitors to have handy as part of visitation training.

Before the Visit
- Verify address, directions, and time of appointment. Make sure the donor knows *why* you are visiting.

- Know the spending priorities in your parish, and be prepared to discuss the many ministries in the parish.

- Where appropriate or if unsure, check with the rector to inform him or her of the visit, and ask if any *current* pastoral issues might get in the way of the objectives of the visit.

- To build self-confidence, review the brochures and other materials, and reacquaint yourself with any major issues current in parish life.

- Know what customized strategic message you are to deliver during the visit.

During the Visit
- Thank the prospect for taking time to see you. Ask where you should sit and indicate approximately how long you plan to

stay. Ask if the donor has any time constraints. Ask politely if the television or radio can be turned off, as you are distracted by it. (You'd be surprised how common it is to have a television on during a visit.)

- If you don't already know, ask about the donor's family: number of children, where they are living, what they do, grandchildren, etc. Listen to answers.

- Ask the donor about their involvement in the church (how long, where, types of ministry they engaged in) and listen to answers for clues about the donor's ministry passions.

- Keep your message simple. Explain what stewardship is and why it is important to the church. Emphasize how real people are being impacted by the ministry of the church. If you feel comfortable about it, indicate how you support the parish.

- *Ask* the donor for a commitment. Be direct. Hand them the pre-authorized payment form or stewardship pledge form, and demonstrate how to fill out each of the time, talent, and treasure sections of the pledge form. Then don't talk. Be patient and give your donor time to think.

- Recap to summarize the meeting and what you both discussed and agreed upon. Suggest some next steps for a follow-up visit based on what you learned.

- Ask if the donor would like to close in prayer, and listen and honor their response. Don't make the prayer a sales pitch.

After the Visit
- Write a thank-you note.

- Make any follow-up phone calls, deliver to the donor any materials you promised.

- Do a self-evaluation of the visit. What went well? What would you do differently?

Questions for Reflection

1. What elements of the five-point plan could you implement in your parish this year even with limited resources?

2. Who do you need to work with to make this happen?

3. Is your rector committed to a leadership role in the stewardship ministry of your parish? If not, what would be a plan for increasing his or her commitment to stewardship?

4. What are the opportunities for strategic visiting in your parish? (See chapter 9, "An Audit of Parish Stewardship" for ideas.)

9

An Audit of Parish Stewardship

Picture the following scenario. You are sitting at home minding your own business, wolfing back a super-sized bag of dill pickle potato chips and a Diet Coke float, and watching the Atlanta Braves lose another deciding game in the divisional playoffs, when the phone rings. You pick up the receiver and curse yourself under your breath for not spending the money on call display. It's the rector of your local Anglican parish and she wants you to take on leadership of the stewardship ministry in the parish.

Because the Braves's pitiful offense has lulled you into a trance, you are not quick enough on your feet. Having no reasonable excuse ready at your fingertips, you hang up the phone and it hits you—you have just agreed to be the stewardship chair for the parish. Over the next couple days you get used to the idea, and by week's end you are even a little excited as you recall your rector's glowing compliments about why you are the only person right for the job. Besides, you have nothing else to do with your spare time now that the Braves are swinging golf clubs instead of baseball bats.[5]

So where do you start? A logical first step would be to try to get a handle on the state of stewardship in your parish. Announce to leadership that you are going to undertake a parish stewardship

---

5 Don't think for a moment that I am bitter about the fall performance of the Braves come playoff time!

audit and ask for their support in this initiative. I would recommend that, in order to proceed with an audit of the state of stewardship in the parish, you work with the envelope secretary to compile the following information.

- Quintile analysis of giving to the operating budget that divides the parish up into five groups—each containing 20% of givers in descending order. So, for example, in a parish with 100 identifiable givers, you would receive a report that would show the giving levels of the top twenty households, the next 20%, etc.
- The number of identifiable givers on the parish list. (This would include envelope holders, pre-authorized payment (PAP) givers, and one-time givers who write an annual check and are identifiable.)
- Average gift per identifiable giver.
- Two-year trend showing this information.
- The number of households utilizing the PAP program and the gift levels for those households.
- A summary of all other revenue sources, with an explanation of those sources.

Through the US Census Bureau you can obtain figures on median household income for your area. This information is usually available for households within a four- to five-mile radius of your church. This data will enable you to make some ballpark estimates of the percentage of their income that people are donating to the parish. For instance, if the median household income is $40,000 in your immediate area and the average gift per identifiable giver is $850 per year, then you can guesstimate that the average gift is approximately 2.1% of income. This will help you to calculate what percentage of proportionate giving you will need to move people toward, in order to meet the ministry needs of the parish.

As you continue to prepare your audit, you will benefit from knowing the response to past Capital Campaigns. If there are any records of past Capital Campaigns—amount raised, average gift, participation levels (that is, percentage of identifiable givers supporting campaign)—that would be helpful. A stewardship audit should also look at endowment funds and assess their quality (that is, size, restricted monies versus unrestricted).

The audit then needs to review the frequency and quality of stewardship education in the parish.

- Have there been any Lenten or other adult education studies on stewardship in the last five years?
- How often is stewardship addressed during sermons?
- Is narrative budgeting part of the parish culture?
- Has stewardship education been addressed in parish newsletters, vestry reports, or parish meetings?
- Is there a culture of pledging in the parish?

You will also want to get a sense of Planned Giving issues in the parish. You might create a response card and put it in pew bulletins for four consecutive Sunday mornings, asking people to fill out the card and indicate if they have remembered to allocate a bequest to the parish in their wills. Besides giving you an audit of the level of Planned Giving in the parish, this can also give you leads for future Planned Giving initiatives.

Finally, you will need a sense of past stewardship initiatives. Look for any documentation or collective memory on when intentional stewardship programs were run and what type of stewardship recipes were utilized.

Then you will want to pull this information together. Invite the parish council or corporation to look at the data with you. Schedule a meeting to discuss input from the audit and to reach a consensus on possible action suggested by the audit. By the conclusion of that meeting you should have a consensus on how you can proceed and an idea of what resources (human or otherwise) you will need to begin the ministry of stewardship in the parish.

A word to the wise—don't try to do too much all at once. The reason for taking an audit is to help you focus your thinking and prioritize the stewardship needs of the parish. The audit should identify where you need to concentrate your effort. As you make progress against your top stewardship priorities, you will develop the momentum and wider ownership across the parish to address secondary priorities.

Questions for Consideration

1. Who are the people who can assist you in completing a stewardship audit of your parish?

2. Who will need to be part of the conversation where you set stewardship priorities for the parish?

3. When will the Atlanta Braves finally win the World Series?

10

A Case Study of a Parish Getting It Right!

In this chapter, I present a study of a very successful, large suburban parish. I am fully aware that there are very few parishes that will be able to identify with the parish of St. Christopher's because of its size. I urge the reader to look beyond the size of the parish and focus on how it handles the logistics of stewardship, and how its theology of baptismal ministry and Christian stewardship informs that approach. I present this case study because the parish was not always the size it is now. Attention to stewardship has been a huge factor in its growth. Maybe implementing a few of their ideas will stretch your parish in positive ways.

Enabling a Spirituality of Abundance

A Case Study

St. Christopher's Anglican Church in Burlington, Ontario, is not your average Anglican parish. In the past ten years it has doubled in size and has grown from a stable parish into a dynamic, spiritually vibrant, outward-looking community of faith that is an example of faithfulness and mission. St. Christopher's has grown from a mid-sized parish to a large parish. Despite its size, it can serve as a useful example for smaller parishes.

As you read this case study, note how principles of Christian stewardship are woven into the tapestry of parish life. Their recently retired rector defines stewardship as "How we manage the love of God."

Some Basic Parish Statistics

- There are 675 households on the parish list.

- Of these households, 475 give regularly and at least monthly, and 525 receipts are issued annually to encompass occasional and one-time givers.

- 150 households process their donation through a pre-authorized payment (PAP) program. Donors are able to give via post-dated checks, monthly automatic withdrawal, or through automatic VISA card monthly deductions. These PAP households represent 32% of identifiable givers.

- In the past ten years the annual operating budget of the parish has doubled from $240,000 per year to $540,000 per year.

- The annual gift per identifiable giver has grown in the past five years from an average of $600 per household to an average of $1,100 per household.

- There is *no collection plate* passed during worship. However, there is a box at each of the two entrances to the worship space with signs saying that donations are welcome.

During the past 10 years the parish participated in two major Capital Campaigns. The first saw $1,000,000 raised for facilities expansion and $350,000 raised over five years for a diocesan Capital Campaign. The past rector promoted a standard of $1,000 per household as a barometer of the minimum level of the annual operating budget.

Parish Ethos

At St. Christopher's there is a strong emphasis on baptismal ministry that flows through parish life. To become a member of the parish one *must* actually join the parish. Membership includes a commitment of time and treasure from day one. This is a common element in most successful stewardship parishes. Membership includes Christian stewardship, and a new member hears this message immediately. In the membership pamphlet newcomers are encouraged to give 2% of income to the ministry of the parish and to work over time to increase that percentage.

Complimenting this emphasis on the duties of membership is a thorough program of hospitality. The parish works hard to ensure that every worshipper is greeted on the way in and on the way out of worship.

Vibrant worship is critical to the success of stewardship education at St. Christopher's. There is a sense that worship empowers and engages people to take up their baptismal ministry. Prayer, Bible study, and the parish web site all reinforce this fundamental cornerstone of the parish's culture. The parish believes strongly that there is a direct link between givings and worship attendance—not a new insight, but an important one.

The parish teaches that we are all on a journey to become "mature Christians." The corporate life of the parish faith community involves modeling faithfulness to the world at large—faith community modeling to civil community. All members are encouraged to take ownership of, and involvement in, the ministry of the parish. The parish actively seeks to be inclusive of young people. Every member over the age of sixteen is asked to fill out a personal profile, and is included on the parish list as a unique household unit.

Stewardship Education at St. Christopher's

The parish emphasizes the stewardship of time. People are encouraged to tithe their time. Regardless of personal economic situation, we all have the 24 hours in our day; and by tithing our time we come to fulfill our baptismal ministry. Both ministry and mission evolve from our role as Christian stewards. The parish has learned that promoting the tithing of time encourages people to respond and to get more involved in its ministry.

An important part of stewardship education at St. Christopher's involves challenging parishioners regularly to *self-examination* of how they give their time and treasure. Every Sunday the pew bulletin contains some notice about either stewardship or Planned Giving. The past rector's sermons were normally spiced with challenges about how parishioners can use their time, talent, and treasure to be the people of God in the world.

By most Anglican standards, the parish stewardship committee is large. The "best givers" are usually on the committee—not only the best financial givers, but also the people with limited financial resources who are effective stewards of their personal time and talent. To emphasize the importance of stewardship in the life of the faith community, the stewardship committee reports directly to the corporation instead of to the parish council. At least one warden attends every stewardship meeting.

The parish has been guided and influenced by ground-breaking work done in the field of stewardship education by the Roman Catholic parish of St. Francis of Assisi in Wichita, Kansas. That parish has an excellent stewardship web site that is user friendly and easily accessible. It is particularly helpful for parishes "getting started." That web site is <http://www.stfranciswichita.com/stewardship/development.asp?f=home>.

St. Christopher's has been employing narrative budgeting for ten years. It tells the story of the unfolding parish ministry and models the gospel story to the wider community. Every household on the parish list gets a copy of the Narrative Budget every year.

Intentional stewardship efforts focus on understanding the different stages where people are in their Christian journey. For stewardship purposes, the parish list is divided into three groups of people—the "core," "supporters," and "occasionals." Every year each of these three groups receives a letter, and all are encouraged to examine their personal giving. The letter includes enclosures of the annual operating budget and the Narrative Budget document.

The core parishioners—150 PAP givers—receive a letter with a request to examine their tithing of time and to prayerfully consider increasing their giving. The supporters, or weekly and monthly envelope users—the second group—are encouraged to examine their giving and to consider moving to become PAP givers. The occasional givers—the third group—receive a letter asking them to become more involved in the worship and fellowship of the parish. This overall methodology employs classic fund-raising "moves management." Donors are cultivated and encouraged to "move inward" toward deeper investment in, and involvement with, the organization and its mission.

The parish does not import a "recipe" stewardship program but remains intentional in implementing its own recipe. In 2000 each of the three groups received an invitation to attend an evening sherry party to learn about the Narrative Budget and the ministry of the parish. And in 2001 each of the groups were invited separately to three different Saturday luncheons to nurture their awareness and involvement in the parish and its mission.

One program that was particularly successful in the early years of the parish's growth spurt was a program called "Pledge to Yourself." All members of the parish were asked to fill out a pledge card and to send it to the rector in a sealed envelope. They were promised that the envelope would remain sealed and *not* be opened by anyone. The following October all households were mailed their unopened pledge card and invited, in a letter with a statement of year-to-date givings, to open it and see how they were doing against the promise they had made to themselves. This was a highly successful and particularly useful way to introduce pledging in a parish that did not have a culture of pledging.

As noted earlier, St. Christopher's does not pass a collection plate at any of its services of worship. This policy was introduced five years ago, and during this timeframe the average gift per giver increased from $600 to $1,100. The parish noticed a small dip in income when the policy was first introduced, but that dip lasted only six weeks and corrected itself within the same calendar year.

The rationale for not passing the plate was based on two vital principles of Christian life. The first is the Christian imperative to be a people of hospitality to visitors. The second is the ongoing theme of St. Christopher's stewardship education to rely on the responsibility of *members* to support the ministry of the faith community. The decision created many opportunities for intentional instruction about "bringing your gift" to the Lord, as opposed to the traditional Anglican practice where the church "comes to you" and asks for your gift.

The past rector firmly believes that any move to return to a weekly passing of the collection plate would leave the current parishioners very upset. This approach accords with the understanding that education is the most important part of stewardship. Dispensing with the collection plate has released visitors from the feeling that they have to contribute and has created many pastoral opportunities for people to engage the rector in conversations about this giving policy.

Moving Forward

St. Christopher's parish understands that there are many areas where it could improve. Parishioners have identified a major need to involve young people more (fifteen- to thirty-year-olds). The parish wants to create more vitality in its worship life and to strengthen the feeling of community through more intentional fellowship events, so that the process of making disciples and educating stewards will continue to evolve naturally.

There is a sense of celebration about the abundant blessings the parish has experienced as it has grown so dramatically. The people understand themselves as a community of hope and celebration.

Case Study Discussion Questions

1. What is St. Christopher's doing that you are *already* doing in your parish?

2. What is St. Christopher's doing that you could implement in your parish?

3. Is there a process for becoming a member of your parish? What is that process?

4. How would you implement a process whereby you are able to identify the "better givers" of time and treasure in your parish?

5. Does the rector know the giving habits and annual offerings of your entire parish? Do you believe the rector should know this information?

6. Can you identify stumbling blocks that would get in the way of moving forward with more intentional stewardship education in your parish?

PART THREE

PLANNED GIVING: STEWARDSHIP OF OUR ACCUMULATED ASSETS

Planned Giving Foreword

The Stewardship and Financial Development Committee of the Anglican Diocese of Niagara launched a parish-based Planned Giving program in the spring of 2002. The goal of the program was to train parish Planned Giving representatives in every parish in Niagara. As part of that launch, committee members spent the better part of a year developing a comprehensive Planned Giving manual to guide parish representatives. That manual is called *Planting Mustard Seeds*. As principal author of the manual, I have borrowed heavily from its text in this section of the stewardship handbook. My thanks to the committee for their work on the manual, their input into the original chapters reflected in this section, and their inspirational passion for the ministry of Planned Giving.

11

A Theological Framework for the Ministry of Planned Giving

Planned Giving is about Stewardship

My job with the Diocese of Niagara has frequently taken me into parishes to preach about stewardship and Planned Giving. On those occasions I have wanted to joke about Planned Giving and the biblical tithe. If I had the intestinal fortitude to tell it, the joke would go something along the lines of, "You didn't tithe in life, why not tithe your estate in death?" Wouldn't that make a great advertisement in the diocesan newspaper? Of course, the bishop would have to install a few extra phone lines to take the complaints that would inundate the office.

This reference to the tithe recognizes that Planned Giving is ultimately about stewardship of the gifts that God has given us. It highlights the point that stewardship of God's creation is a lifelong endeavor. We are given resources in abundance during life to utilize, share, and then pass on. The theological framework for stewardship presented earlier in this manual applies equally to Planned Giving and to other forms of stewardship. They all assume the same theological grounds for responding to God.

Having said that, I would like to offer an additional theological perspective from which to view the ministry of Planned Giving.

Planned Giving as Jubilee

Ancient Israel held the principle of Jubilee as sacred. In Leviticus 25 and 27 (especially verses 16 to 25), and in Numbers 36 verse 4, the principle of Jubilee is articulated. Every fifty years the people of Israel were commanded by the law to return land and other property to the original owners, to redistribute wealth so that the poor might have a share in the bounty of the Lord.

Jubilee laws called on Israel to restore an equitable distribution of land and property, and there is much evidence in the ancient world that this redistribution was reality, not fiction. Some scholars doubt whether the fifty-year cycle was actually practised in Israel. Evidence suggests that a seven-year Jubilee cycle was the norm. According to the biblical concept of Jubilee, God has a plan to provide equitably for all. The world, it is recognized, will continue to veer off into imbalance, but devoted Christians can take concrete action to proclaim and demonstrate the truth that the whole world, and all that is in it, is from God and owned by God, not by us.

We know that God moves our hearts to give. Certainly we want our family members to be taken care of, but we also want to give. Throughout our lives as members of the church we are regular supporters of its ministry and display consistent generosity over time. Usually giving derives from our cash flow or family operational budgets. The Planned Gift comes, almost always, from accumulated assets.

In many ways the Planned Gift can be seen from a theological perspective as a form of individually declared Jubilee—returning personal resources to God for redistribution to others who need them. But there is also a sacred trust at stake. The donor trusts that the church, being faithful to the concept of Jubilee, will redistribute the assets, often acquired over a lifetime, to ministry that honors the passions and intentions of the donor. Thus, through our Planned Gift we become agents of Jubilee together—true stewards of the gifts of God.

All of this becomes possible as we move forward in our spiritual journeys from scarcity to abundance, to the life that Jesus calls us to, and the inner peace and freedom that it brings.

12

Planned Giving 101

The kingdom of God ... is like a mustard seed, which, when
sown upon the ground, is the smallest of all the seeds on earth;
yet when it is sown it grows up and becomes the greatest of all
shrubs, and puts forth large branches, so that the birds of the
air can make nests in its shade. (Mark 4:31–32)

Planting Mustard Seeds

The ministry of Planned Giving takes patience above all. You may
toil for years in this ministry and *never* see the results. But like the
mustard seed, your ministry may grow from the smallest of seeds
to become the greatest of shrubs. This chapter has been structured
as an easy-to-follow primer for parish leaders and Planned Giving
volunteers, to enable you to move forward with Planned Giving in
your parish.

Planned Giving is a vital component of any charity's financial
development strategy. Since the mid-1990s, virtually every significant
charity has seen the wisdom of putting major resources into developing a sustainable Planned Giving program. Starting a Planned Giving
program requires commitment, and it requires patience. Most charities agree that it takes five to seven years before the fruits of attention
to Planned Giving begin to be noticed. During those early years there
may be occasional gifts, but they will be rare.

Individual parish leaders who have taken up this ministry need to be patient yet steadfast in their commitment to the ministry of Planned Giving. It is not a ministry that will deliver instant gratification, if one measures progress solely on the number of gifts received by the parish. This is not to say that there aren't many satisfactions and rewards, even in the early years.

Certainly the Planned Gift is extremely important to individual donors. It often represents much more than just a donation to a favored charity or church. For many, the Planned Gift symbolizes several meaningful issues surrounding the donor's life. A bequest or gift later in life is a way of declaring one's priorities, of giving impetus to a ministry, of making an impact on an institution that has been an important part of a donor's history.

Planned Gifts bring meaning to life. They represent a concrete expression of what a person feels their life has been about. The Planned Giving ministry is very sacred—and usually very pastoral. Many donors feel that arranging a Planned Gift is part of the unfinished business that they must complete to be at peace as the later years approach. By helping donors to make this gift we become agents of peace to them.

So, as you can see, the ministry of Planned Giving can be very rewarding. It is a way to work on behalf of your parish to help secure the future of important ministries that are an essential element of the parish—its self-identity and its identity in the local community. Planned Gifts also secure the financial resources to help sustain important programs at the diocesan and national church levels.

One final word before you flip these pages and begin your study of this chapter. Many people new to Planned Giving find themselves somewhat intimidated by what they perceive to be a very complex subject. Let's face it, we are not all up to date on the latest tax implications of charitable giving, the nuances of gift annuities, and the management of endowment funds, and some of us quake at the thought of trying to understand the workings of charitable remainder trusts.

The good news is simply this: You do not have to be a trained chartered accountant, financial planner, or estate lawyer to engage a vital and vibrant Planned Giving ministry. This section of the stewardship primer is designed to give you the basic tools you need to feel comfortable in discussing Planned Gifts with donors. It is also very clear about the need for donors to connect with their own financial advisors.

There are resources at your synod office to which you can refer donors for assistance, if complex gifting situations arise. So relax. *Good Planned Giving programs thrive on relationship building.* Credibility, integrity, diligence, and pastoral sensitivity are the lifeblood of Planned Giving. The technical expertise of the Planned Giving representative, in reality, has very minimal impact on the success of a parish program.

Basics of Planned Giving

There are three components to any Planned Gift. Planned Giving is the process of designing charitable gifts so that a donor realizes *philanthropic* intentions while also maximizing *tax benefits* and other *financial planning* objectives.

Any gift made with forethought to the benefit of both the institution and the donor is technically a Planned Gift. There are two types of Planned Gifts—present and deferred. Present gifts include donations of cash, securities, charitable gift annuities, or property, for example. Deferred gifts most often comprise bequests, but can also be gifts of life insurance, or proceeds of a Registered Retirement Savings Plan or Registered Retirement Investment Fund, or a charitable trust.

Deferred gifts can be revocable or irrevocable. The majority of Planned Gifts to churches are deferred, but this does not have to be the case. Many donors make outright Planned Gifts of cash or securities because this meets their philanthropic, tax, and financial planning needs. Gifts can be restricted or unrestricted with regard to the charity's end use of the proceeds of the gift.

The Climate for Planned Giving

In our society, there has been an increasing movement, driven by governments wanting to download responsibility, to transfer social service programs to the not-for-profit sector. This has allowed governments to promote tax relief for voters. By stepping into the void created by such shifts in public policy, private donors have shown both the financial ability and the altruistic willingness to fund much-needed social programs. Many on the margins of society would otherwise find themselves in even deeper financial and social distress. Charities have seen their workload increase and have discovered the positive impact that Planned Giving programs can have on funding their programs.

The current climate is also favorable to Planned Giving because of shifting demographic trends. The population group most likely to make Planned Gifts is expanding dramatically. Approximately one out of eight persons is now over the age of sixty-five, and that proportion will increase to one out of five by the middle of this century.

You may have heard a great deal of talk about a much-anticipated transfer of wealth from the current generation to the next over the next two decades. Some economists estimate that 30 trillion dollars will change hands in the United States alone. Actually, this transfer of wealth has already begun, and many already well-to-do baby boomers are finding themselves with sizable inheritances passed on by the very frugal generation that went before them.

Currently, most bequests received by charities come from donors born in the 1920s and 1930s. There will be a temporary slowdown for a time, but then a huge increase as baby boomers (usually with much smaller families and greater wealth to leave to charity) begin to pass away.

For members of the Anglican community, Planned Gifts represents a very different method of giving compared to past practices in the church. For most of their lives, Anglicans have given to the church from income and cash flow. However, a Planned Gift is almost always the gift of an asset or accumulated assets. This involves a major shift in the psychological dynamics motivating a gift, a shift we must make an effort to understand if we are truly to be empathetic and of service to our potential donors.

As many charitable institutions in society create Planned Giving offices, donors are becoming more and more aware of the Planned Giving opportunity in estate and financial planning. This increased awareness will lead to greater acceptance and increased usage of Planned Gifts to the church, which in turn will exert pressure on parishes to put clear, well-constructed endowment programs in place to receive donations. More about this later.

Donor Motivations

As one might expect, tax relief plays a major role in gift planning, especially for donors in higher tax brackets. For all donors, however, *the largest motivator is a desire to support a favorite charity and make a difference in the work of that charity.* We must not lose sight of this. The good news is that Canadians give more to religious institutions than to all other charities combined. Additionally, churchgoers are statistically more philanthropic than the population at large.

When we talk to donors, we must remember that they may have a stronger need to *give* to our church than we as a church have to *receive* their gift. Their empathy for the needy is served by the charity.

Perhaps the most important motivation behind a gift is the quest for meaning. Most people want to believe that their lives have made a difference, that they will be remembered with appreciation, and that their values will somehow endure. Donors may wish to perpetuate an individual or family name. Providing a donor with the opportunity to leave something of lasting worth is an important way we can serve them.

Besides a desire to support a favorite charity, one of the major factors motivating a Planned Gift is the relationship the donor has with the representative of the charity. Fostering personal relationships is an important part of Planned Giving. We have relationships with our parishioners that most secular charities could never hope to cultivate. This gives us a dramatic advantage as the church.

Some Background Information about Charitable Giving
- Charitable giving is $248.52 billion annually in the U.S..

- Planned Giving is approximately $19.80 billion annually in the U.S.

Distribution of Planned Giving Gifts by Type
- Annuities   10%

- Life Insurance   10%

- Trusts   5%

- Bequests   75%

- Total   100%

In the church these figures are even more pronounced. Bequests can be as high as 90% of a parish's Planned Gift donations.

More Donor Dynamics
- 75% of donors have *not* notified the charity that they have included in their wills.

- 37% of bequest donors designate only *one* charity in their will.

- Religious groups are recipients of just over 50% of all charitable gifts in Canada.

- 92% of bequest donors do *not* change the bequest provision once it is in the will.
- 62% of Planned Gift donors are women. (Women usually outlive their spouses and are the eventual distributors of the family's accumulated wealth.)

Types of Planned Gifts

The following section will review some of the basic characteristics of the various Planned Giving vehicles available to donors, which include

- bequests;
- charitable gift annuities;
- life insurance policies;
- gifts of residual interest in properties;
- charitable remainder trusts;
- outright gifts of cash, property, or securities.

When we start talking about these specific types of gifts, many Planned Giving volunteers begin to feel overwhelmed. This reaction is totally understandable but unnecessary. The intent of this brief summary is not to make you an expert—we always recommend donors consult their own financial planners—but to give you a basic understanding of donor options when contemplating a Planned Gift.

1. Bequests

- We first need to understand that people do their estate planning on their own timetables and not on our schedules.

- Therefore, it is important to always be asking—frequently and in a tasteful, low-key way—so that our church is on people's minds when they set out to do their estate planning.

- Our first task is to encourage parishioners to write a will. Many people avoid writing a will because they see themselves as too busy or too young, or they are in denial about death. Others think making a will is costly or complicated.

- Most clergy can tell you of the pastoral disasters they face frequently when a person has died unexpectedly without having written a will. Wills are extremely important, if only for this pastoral reason. Make no mistake about it—*the lack of a will can tear families apart!* Clergy see more of this than most lay people imagine. We do our membership a wonderful service by encouraging them to write a will and keep it up-to-date.

- Then we must ask them to remember the church in their will. Often people tell us that the church was left out of a will because it never asked to be included!

- For the Christian, a will is very satisfying to write. It is a proclamation of faith and a statement of who you are and what you value most in life.

- A will brings a donor peace of mind. Encouraging a fellow parishioner to make a will is a gift you can give them.

- Statistics show that, when a person includes a charity in their will, 92% of the time they leave that charity in the will and in any future revisions to the will. This is exciting news for charities.

- Often donors want to direct the use of their bequest. We can encourage them to support the church by asking gentle questions about the areas of the parish (or diocese's) ministry that is important to them. In Niagara Diocese the Anglican Church Ministries Foundation has created several funds to which donors can direct their bequests. These include endowments for youth ministry, outreach, education and training, evangelism, divinity students, and clergy in transition. Your parish may have separate funds in some of these areas or a parish general endowment fund. In most instances we prefer that donors put as few restrictions on a gift as possible. But their interests and passions are ignored at our peril. Listening is an important element of the ministry of Planned Giving. When we meet with donors, they will usually give us clues about their passions in ministry. Honoring these passions, motivations, and intentions creates a positive climate for the ministry of Planned Giving in a parish.

Sample Bequest Language
"I give to my parish/(diocese), *Name, Diocese, Province,* the sum of $100,000 to be used according to (my wishes) under the direction of the corporation of the parish *(bishop of the diocese)."*

Or

"I give to my parish/(diocese), *Name, Diocese, Province,* all of my shares in XYZ Company to be used for (state usage) under the direction of the corporation of the parish *(bishop of the diocese)."*

Or

"I give to my parish/(diocese), *Name, Diocese, Province,* 10% of my estate to be used according to my wishes for the furtherance of _____ *(youth ministry, evangelism, major capital improvements, expansion, or repairs and maintenance)* under the direction of the corporation of the parish *(bishop of the diocese)."*

2. Charitable Gift Annuities

What is a Gift Annuity?

- A gift annuity is a contract under which a charity, in return for a transfer of cash or another property, agrees to pay a fixed sum of money for a period measured by one or two lives.

How do Gift Annuities work?

- In exchange for your gift, the Anglican Church (either the national church or the diocese) buys you a lifetime annuity from a licensed insurance company or the national church.

- What is left of your contribution after the church buys the annuity becomes your gift to the church.

- The amount of your annuity depends on your age and the size of your contribution. The rate will usually be much higher than what you get from your current investments *and* the rate is guaranteed.

- If a donor is married, he or she may choose an annuity that continues as long as either spouse is alive.

- A gift annuity brings another bonus. Depending on the age of the donor when he or she takes out the annuity, a part or all of each payment to the donor will be income tax free. At the time of the donation the charity will issue a receipt that will result in a tax credit to the donor.

Donors like Gift Annuities

- Over the past thirty years gift annuities have become very popular among donors. Many seniors like annuities because these gifts provide a way to contribute substantially to their church in their lifetime.

- Some reasons for this are
  - attractive rates of return promote better cash flow for donors;
  - guaranteed rates provide protection from market fluctuations;
  - gift annuities provide the peace of mind of regular payments for life, and remove the worry of many seniors that their investments may not last as long as they do;
  - gift annuities enable support for the church at much higher levels than may have been contemplated, while at the same time protecting cash flow and showing a donor's assets at work.

3. Gifts of Life Insurance

- Next to bequests, life insurance is the most common deferred gift received by Canadian charities.

- As family needs change and children grow, many donors find themselves holding policies that are no longer essential to family financial planning. These policies have, in effect, become idle assets. They can be used to create a win/win situation for financial tax planning and for the Anglican Church.

- There are several ways to gift life insurance to the church:
  - donors can donate a policy they no longer need;
  - they can buy a new policy as a gift and pay the premiums;
  - they can donate other assets to the church and use life insurance to replace the value of those assets for their heirs.

Transferring Ownership of a Paid-Up Policy
- The donor is entitled to a donation receipt for the total cash surrender value at the time of the gift. This allows the donor the

satisfaction of giving the church a larger than usual gift from assets instead of from income.

- The gift of a paid-up life insurance policy is the equivalent of an outright gift of cash. This is because the church can, if it chooses, immediately surrender the policy for cash. Most often, however, the church will retain the policy until the passing of the insured donor and then collect the full death benefit.

Transferring Ownership of an Existing Policy on which Premiums are Owing
- The donor is entitled to a tax receipt for the cash surrender value of the policy when the policy is transferred to the church, and also for subsequent premium payments.

- Gifts of life insurance policies on which premiums are still owing are most suitable for donors who have the cash flow from income to continue to make premium payments. The gift allows them to make a larger than normal gift at an annual cost not prohibitive to their life style.

Purchase of a New Policy Naming the Anglican Church as Owner
- A donor who has some discretionary income but cannot afford to contribute from existing capital assets can buy a life insurance policy, name the church as owner, and pay the premiums. The donor gets a tax credit and a donation receipt amounting to 45% of each premium paid.

Gifts of life insurance are truly a way to make idle assets work or give larger than usual gifts out of cash flow without touching a donor's asset base.

4. Gifts of a Life Estate

- In making a gift of life estate, a donor irrevocably transfers property to the church. This property is usually a principal residence, cottage, or rental property. The donor retains the use of the property for his or her lifetime (and often for the duration of the spouse's lifetime), and then ownership reverts to the church.

- While the donor lives on the property, they are responsible for maintenance, taxes, insurance, and other expenses as stipulated in the agreement with the church.

- A gift of residual interest in property is very attractive to many donors and to your church. It permits the donor to make a very substantial gift to the church *and* obtain a very large tax benefit. The disadvantage of this type of gift is that it is irrevocable and donors lose some (but not total) control of their asset(s). This type of gift works best for donors seventy-five years of age and older.

Donors receive a donation receipt that will reduce their income taxes, and also maintain use of their asset for the duration of their life.

5. Charitable Remainder Trusts

- The charitable remainder trust is a gifting vehicle for donors who have assets they would like to give the church at some point; however, they need the income these assets generate while they are still alive.

- With a charitable remainder trust, the donor places an asset or assets in trust for the church, but continues to receive the income they provide. The trust can be set up to be transferred to the charity at death or after a specified period of time. The charity issues the donor a tax receipt for the year the gift is made. That receipt represents the value today of the future gift. It is actuarially computed, and determined from the amount contributed, the age of the donor, and a current discount rate.

- The most common assets placed in trust in this type of gifting vehicle are real estate and securities. Often these investments have appreciated and incurred capital gains. When a donor transfers property to a remainder trust, income taxes that would have been paid on the capital gain are cut by 50%.

- The charitable remainder trust also removes the asset from the donor's estate, which is a selling point to some donors who want heirs to receive the full estate but also want to provide for a favorite charity.

The charitable remainder trust is a versatile tool that can be tailored to an individual donor's specific financial situation. The donor designates the trustee who will administer it. Because the trust is irrevocable after it has been established, the donor should always seek the guidance of independent legal and financial advisors.

6. Outright Gifts

- An outright gift of cash or property puts the full amount of a gift to the Anglican Church to work immediately, providing vital support for the church's mission and ministry. Donors get the satisfaction of seeing their gifts at work right away.

- Many donors will want to make gifts in cash or by credit card.

- Non-cash assets, such as securities and real estate, can also become outright gifts. The donor receives a tax receipt and a tax credit. And, for gifts of securities where there has been a capital gain, the donor avoids significant tax on the gain and always receives a net tax savings.

7. Gifts of Securities

Securities include stocks, bonds, bills, warrants, and futures traded on approved stock exchanges in Canada and certain other countries. They also include mutual funds. In the last few years, giving securities to the church has become a very popular way of making a gift.

Donors will be taxed according to the prevailing laws of the state in which they reside.

You may have many donors who have highly appreciated stocks and mutual funds in your portfolio. In the past, many people hesitated to give such assets to the church because of the tax payable on the capital gain. Now that the taxable gain on giving these assets is only half what it was before, there is a strong incentive to give. Donors may own securities that are not expected to perform as well as they have in the past, and may be thinking of selling them. Donors may be well advised, if planning a gift of cash to the church, to keep the cash and give the securities, rather than sell the securities and give the cash proceeds.

Benefits to Donors for Giving Securities
- Donors receive a charitable receipt for the fair market value of his securities. In the case of stocks and bonds, fair market value is the closing price on the date of the gift. For mutual funds, it is the "bid price" on the date of the gift.

- Donors will be taxed on a percentage of the capital gain, depending on the state in which they live. This percentage, however, will be lower than the one they would have paid had they sold the securities.

- Securities gifts often allow donors to make a much more substantial gift to the church than they might otherwise have been able to do. It also gives them the satisfaction of seeing their gift make a significant impact on the life of the church.

And Now for a Little Twist
Some donors resist giving large gifts of securities because a significant asset is removed from the estate and will no longer be available for their heirs. Did you know that many donors use the tax savings from this kind of gift to buy a life insurance policy on themselves as wealth replacement insurance? The death benefit payout to the

estate replaces the charitable gift of securities, and the overall value of the assets of the estate remains unchanged.

The donor receives the satisfaction of making a significant gift, the church receives that significant gift, and the heirs of the estate are protected financially. In fact, the value of the estate for the heirs is larger, because the estate pays no capital gains tax on the life insurance death benefit, but it would pay capital gains tax on the securities, had they not been gifted!

Planned Giving 101: A Final Word

As a parish Planned Giving committee volunteer, you are *not* expected to be an expert on these many vehicles or tools for making a Planned Gift. This section of the primer has been written solely so that you will be aware of the variety of gifting opportunities available. Your parish is not asking you to put yourself in a position of offering financial or tax planning advice. The role of the parish Planned Giving volunteer is to provide a quality invitation to donor prospects to consider a Planned Gift to the Anglican Church, to educate donor prospects about the variety of vehicles available, and to create and sustain awareness of the Planned Giving opportunity in the parish.

If you prepare Planned Giving brochures or other printed materials, these should not be represented as constituting legal or financial advice. We encourage every donor to seek professional, legal, estate planning and financial advice before deciding on a course of action. If you feel that a donor is asking you for expert advice, explain that you have not been trained to provide such advice. To protect yourself and your parish, call the diocesan Planned Giving coordinator in your synod office and share the situation. They will be happy to work with you and the donor to ensure that donor, parish, and diocesan interests are protected.

13

Is Your Parish Ready to Begin a Planned Giving Program?

Several elements that signal readiness to begin a Planned Giving program have been identified by Planned Giving professionals for your parish leadership to consider. Your parish is probably ready to move forward with Planned Giving if most of these factors describe your current situation:

- a significant number of your members are over the age of fifty;

- you are perceived by the community to have a long-term future;

- you have a significant number of donors who currently give you more than $100 per year;

- you possess an ability to invest human resources in Planned Giving and be patient for a future return;

- you have committed leadership who will stick with the program and make their own Planned Gifts.

I suspect that most parishes in the Episcopal and Canadian Anglican churches meet these criteria.

There are two other key factors involved in assessing parish readiness to start Planned Giving programs. First, your parish leadership must work to assure donors that you have the procedures in place to manage investment funds. Donors want to know that their gift is being managed wisely and will have a long life.

You will need to communicate how parish leaders are faithfully stewarding the parish's investments. I recommend a stand-alone annual "Investments Report" to vestry that addresses the following issues:

- balances of all funds and investment income in the previous year(s);
- how is money invested?;
- how transparent is the investment process?;
- what checks and balances are in place to insure donors' are protected?;
- who is managing parish investment funds?;
- how much flexibility do parish leaders have to spend investment funds?;
- whether any money from investments is being directed to the annual operating budget and, if so, how much and how it is being utilized?;
- what funds are restricted for use in certain ministries?;
- what funds are restricted on access to the principal?;
- what is the process for accessing funds for special parish mega projects?;
- a summary of expenditures for the previous twelve months and verbal commentary on the ministries supported by these expenditures;
- a sense of what expenditures from investments will be made in the current year and what ministries will be supported;

- what opportunities exist to fund extant parish endowment funds or create new memorial/endowment funds?

This report assists the parish Planned Giving representative as a "sales" tool when discussing potential gifts with donors.

The second critical element that needs to be in place in assessing readiness to begin Planned Giving involves putting together a parish "Case for Support." This will be discussed at length in the next chapter.

What Results to Expect

Results are *not* immediate. Like a newly planted orchard, a Planned Giving program takes time to bear fruit. In the early years, the program should be evaluated according to contacts made and expectancies raised, rather than actual gifts received. A program should start generating additional outright gifts by the second year. Count on *six years* elapsing before deferred gifts start to mature in any noticeable fashion.

It is very difficult to get a handle on expectancies. The only truly reliable way is when someone tells a parish leader specifically that they have included the parish in their will, or have made the parish a recipient of a life insurance policy or residual interest. I recommend that each parish distribute a "bequest intentions" card in the pew leaflet at least twice a year to encourage parishioners to declare any expectancies. This practice also raises awareness of the possibility of Planned Giving for those who have not yet made a bequest to the parish.

14

If I Give You My Money, How Will You Spend It?

The Parish Case for Support

When I was nineteen, I got my first full-time job. I was hired to be a territory sales representative for a huge multinational corporation, the Procter and Gamble Company. Then as now, P&G had an almost mythical reputation for the quality of their sales training. It was considered *the* place for a young green kid to learn how to sell. I was excited to land the job and even more impressed with myself as I tooled down the highway in a brand-new company car with only a few miles on it, the upholstery and interior oozing that wonderful new car smell. Not bad for a nineteen-year-old kid!

Much to my shock, they didn't just hand me my briefcase and order pad, and set me loose on an unsuspecting world. I was scheduled into some very rigorous training that lasted at least two months before I was permitted to make my first solo sales call. I had to learn all their policies and procedures, and memorize their pricing, but most of all I had to learn all about the entire product line.

How does any of this relate to Planned Giving you may ask? It's actually vitally relevant. Before you can undertake the ministry of Planned Giving in your parish, you need to be able to answer the question, *If I give you my money, how will you spend it?* To send a volunteer out into the living rooms of the parish without being able to answer this question is akin to equipping a sales representative with an expense account, company car, order pad, but no product to sell!

The quality work that goes into Planned Giving can be all for naught if your parish visitors cannot answer that question. To leave our visitors unequipped when it comes to a well-thought-out response to this question is just plain unacceptable. Rest assured, the local hospitals, United Way campaigns, universities, and other wellness charities can answer exactly how they would deploy donor money.

Today's sophisticated donors want to know how the church plans to spend their money. Remember that a Planned Gift is almost always sourced from accumulated wealth and not from annual donor cash flow. Because of this, donors are much more concerned that the money be spent prudently and impact the lives of those served by the parish. Donors feel very passionately toward many of a parish's ministries, and they want to know that their passions are being honored.

It is the task of the parish leadership team to support the parish Planned Giving representative in his or her ministry by working together to provide a comprehensive response to this question. We do this by developing a parish "Case for Support" document. This document has three purposes:

1. It articulates the mission of the parish and imagines the shape and scope of that mission in the near-term future, using a five- to fifteen-year window.

2. It thoughtfully lays out compelling reasons for donors to invest in the ministry of the parish, in order to motivate donors.

3. It illustrates how the parish, through fulfilling its mission, will impact the local community and the lives of community members.

In many parishes, there will be a sophisticated, highly developed vision for the future. It will include a mission statement that the congregation has approved and incorporates into parish life, a sense of the priority ministries for development, and a list of the priority ministries for any new funding. In other parishes, there will be work to be done before the fruits of Planned Giving can be maximized.

In today's philanthropic environment, people are too sophisticated to give gifts of any substantive size without the assurance that their gift will be used wisely and have a long life: *If I give you my money, how will you spend it?* There are many dynamics packed into this one little question. When people ask this question, they are really saying that they want their money to be used wisely, to have an impact on the lives of others, to further the goals of the church, and, importantly, not be wasted away, mismanaged, or misspent.

Think of the options available to donors. They can give to a hospital and know their gift will help fund a piece of medical equipment. They can give to a library and know books will be purchased. Today's donors demand the same degree of accountability from the church. They want to see their gifts put to work and make a difference. Other charities have become adept at showing donors how their gifts will be utilized. The church at the parish, diocesan, and national levels must be equally diligent in communicating how gifts will be deployed and accounting to donors after a gift has been made.

Think of donors as investors. They are investing in the church's ministry because they believe it will create a high return in the quality of people's lives. The Case for Support is a form of prospectus inviting investment in ministry rather than securities. When viewed from this perspective, a good deal of planning needs to go into the Case for Support. It is never the work of one individual, and the parish Planned Giving representative must be wary of falling into the trap of taking on this process on his or her own.

If your parish does not have a strategic plan, you may need to champion its development and participate on a parish strategic planning committee. In consultation with the parish corporation, invite people to work with you to set priorities and discuss what you are currently doing well, how you might expand your servant ministry internally and beyond parish doors, and where the parish might best deploy its combined spiritual gifts. Perhaps your synod office has resources and volunteer consultants that can come into the parish and help you develop a strategic plan.

If your parish does have a Strategic Plan, you may wish to ask a warden or the corporation to work with you to help you distill its essential elements into a Case for Support. Put yourself in the shoes of a donor. Ask yourself what questions a donor would have about the parish's future ministry. These may include:

- What is the parish's top priority for the next five years?
- What new programs (youth/children's ministry, seniors' ministry, outreach, worship, etc.) do we foresee the community needing?
- What is our plan for evangelism in the parish?
- How will we market our parish new-member ministry? What will it cost?
- What programs do current endowments fund?
- Where will money be needed in the future?
- Is there a plan (and the necessary funding) to keep the physical facility and office equipment maintained and upgraded over time?
- Are there any long-term plans for physical expansion?
- Does the worship team plan to expand its music ministry, and what are the cost implications for instruments, worship supplies, etc.?
- Will we in the foreseeable future have any incremental employment needs that our current budget cannot cover?

Who we think we are, and where we think we are going, go a long way toward shaping people's perceptions of our church. You must project a high self-image and positive energy. This attitude will become contagious, and donors will catch the enthusiasm and commitment that the framers of the Case for Support have for the church. Show in what ways your parish is strong and progressive. Be honest in your self-assessment of the parish, and that honesty will emerge in your Case for Support. We must be very definitive and unequivocal about where we think our church is going. Only God knows, but we must articulate our vision clearly.

The only valid rationale for doing financial development (Planned Giving) is a strong sense that the church is moving forward and that funding will be needed to help drive this movement. Define what your financial needs are and how funding will make your parish stronger and more effective.

The Case for Support is basically a restatement of the central elements of the strategic plan for the future. It tells donors the major goals of the parish, its game plan for ministry, and the anticipated funding needs. Completing this step helps you communicate the parish's needs to donors. Many donors have specific areas of ministry for which they feel personally passionate. If those passions are reflected in the Case for Support, they will feel more compelled to support the parish with a Planned Gift.

If a donor's personal passions do not intersect with parish long-term goals, the Case for Support provides an opportunity to gently suggest that donors may wish to consider and give primacy to the current needs of the parish (or diocese). But a well-developed case statement will usually speak to everyone's pet passions, because it will reflect plans for the advancement of all parish ministries—youth, outreach, worship, evangelism, parish life, etc.

The Case for Support is a tool to help you sell the concept of making a gift for ministry, a tool to effectively answers donors' questions about how their gifts will be utilized by the church. Time spent up front developing a strong and compelling Case for Support is *essential* to maximizing returns from your parish Planned Giving program. It is from this Case for Support that you can then develop a brochure outlining the reasons for people to consider a Planned Gift.

Testing the Case for Support

The Case for Support should first be tested with a handful of parishioners who may be prospects for a Planned Gift. Show these prospects the brochure, and get feedback on how compelling your case is to them.

The biggest impairment to successful financial development—whether Capital Campaign, Planned Giving, or annual operating budget—is a mission plan that is not compelling. People want to invest their philanthropic dollars in projects that are exciting and will make an impact. Let the people in your test group tell you if your Case for Support "delivers." Ask them how you could make your case more compelling. Are there initiatives that would be more appealing to them; are there initiatives that they think would be even more appealing to others?

When a compelling Case for Support is developed, you are ready to begin in earnest. The sales rep (Planned Giving visitor) now has a persuasive and unique product to sell!

Questions for Consideration

1. What will be the main building blocks in your parish's Case for Support?

2. Who in your parish should be part of the process of pulling the Case for Support together?

3. What procedures or "pockets" do you need to set up to receive gifts and to encourage donors to give to ministries they feel passionate about?

4. How is your parish making a difference in the local community?

15

Job Description for a Parish Planned Giving Chair and the Role of the Rector

In this chapter we look at a potential job description and some of the attributes that would be desirable in the ministry of Planned Giving. If you are a clergy person or parish stewardship chair planning to recruit someone to take on the ministry of Planned Giving in your parish, you may find the following job description and attributes list will help to get you started.

Position Summary

The Parish Planned Giving Representative (PPGR) is a volunteer and almost always a lay person. He or she will be the primary volunteer in a parish responsible for the ministry of Planned Giving. This is a ministry to all members of a parish. The PPGR works with the rector, wardens, parish stewardship committee, and diocesan resource people to maximize the effectiveness of their role.

Ideal Attributes of the PPGR Volunteer

This ministry will appeal to someone who possesses the following attributes:

- has a firm belief in personal stewardship as part of an integrated Christian discipleship;

- has a passion for the future ministry of the parish and the wider church, and a belief in the need to do long-term planning for that ministry;

- has written a will and made provision in that will for a bequest to the Episcopal Church;

- enjoys and is comfortable in public speaking to large and small groups;

- enjoys and is comfortable in one-on-one discussions with individuals about their financial and estate planning;

- has credibility and integrity among the parish at large;

- has the time available to devote up to five to ten hours per month;

- is a good team player and has a good working relationship with the rector;

- is a person of patience, as Planned Giving programs take time to bear fruit;

- has some degree of financial and marketing acumen, though major expertise in this area is not necessary;

- is not afraid to discuss death in a sensitive and pastoral manner with donors.

Important Notes

It is strongly recommended that the Parish Planned Giving Representative undergo a police check. Because the Planned Giving representative's duties often require that they speak with vulnerable elderly people about financial issues in their homes, it is prudent to protect the parish, the representative, and the prospective donor.

This position is *not* recommended for an allied professional (for example, a lawyer, estate planner, or financial planner) who may be perceived, whether fairly or unfairly, to have a potential conflict of

From Scarcity to Abundance

interest in advancing personal business interests by taking on this ministry. Having cautioned you about this possible conflict, I need to mention that many Anglican parishes recruit an allied professional anyway, through a lack of other volunteer resources.

Responsibilities

1. to attend initial training events and annual continuing education workshops (as offered) designed to give the PPGR a basic knowledge base and skills for undertaking this ministry;

2. to act as the primary contact person between the parish and the diocesan or national church Planned Giving office;

3. to act as an information source to parish leadership, keeping them informed about the ministry interests of donors in general;

4. to champion the development of a customized parish Case for Support to market to Planned Giving donor prospects;

5. to create awareness of Planned Giving opportunities among donor prospects and in the parish at large, using materials generated internally and by the diocesan Planned Giving office;

6. to invite individual donors to consider making a Planned Gift to the Episcopal Church;

7. to always act ethically and in accordance with the best interests of the donor and the parish or diocese;

8. to follow up with donors who indicate an interest in making a Planned Gift, and enable them to turn that interest into a commitment.

Term of Position

This is a long-term position in a parish. Because of its unusual nature and the relationships built performing this ministry, most people may want to take this ministry on for a period of at least three years. Of course, as other interested parishioners become involved in the ministry, the term of this position will shorten.

Rewards of Being a Planned Giving Volunteer

There are many rewards and satisfactions in taking on the ministry of Planned Giving in a parish. Many volunteers feel that theirs is one of the more vital ministries in the parish.

- Some volunteers take delight in the knowledge that their ministry has resulted in gifts that help secure the foreseeable financial future and viability of their parish, the diocese, and the church's ministry.

- Some enjoy the important one-to-one contact with shut-ins and others who are no longer physically able to take part in many of the regular activities of the church. Planned Giving visits often help these parishioners to maintain a feeling of belonging and fellowship in the parish community.

- Perhaps one of the greatest rewards derived from the ministry of Planned Giving is the knowledge that one has helped facilitate a sacred gift that allows the donor to feel that they have brought meaning to their life in the act of making the gift.

The Role of the Clergy in Planned Giving

It is a reality that clergy are gatekeepers in most parishes in the Episcopal and Canadian Anglican churches. In many places clergy still have the responsibility and power to set the vision and agenda for the various ministries in a parish. The most important role a clergy person has to play in Planned Giving is to support the ministry and to be regularly heard extolling the virtues of Planned Giving for the long-term health of the parish.

The rector's role can be narrowed to the following general categories:

1. stewardship education in teaching and preaching that includes promoting Planned Gifts as part of overall personal growth in stewardship;

2. emphasis on stewardship and Planned Giving as a valid and vital ministry within the wide array of ministries in parish life;

3. identification and recruitment of Planned Giving parish representatives and/or committee members;

4. identification (and cultivation where appropriate) of potential donors to the Planned Giving representative or stewardship committee;

5. donor pastoral care associated with the consideration of a Planned Gift.

Planned Giving programs work best when they are driven and run by the laity. The central role for the rector is to be overtly supportive and to communicate the benefits to the long-term ministry of the parish by attention to Planned Giving. The rector should encourage the parish representative to attend any available training events. It is also recommended that the rector commission the Planned Giving person or team during worship, and uphold this ministry with ongoing encouragement, recognition, and affirmation.

16

Raising Awareness of
Planned Giving in the Parish

The "mustard seed" for this chapter first appeared in the Planned Giving manual of the Diocese of Niagara and was written by committee chair Gordon Ross. My thanks to Gordon for crafting that chapter, which is the foundation for this chapter.

Potential donors must be aware of Planned Giving opportunities within the church when they are considering their financial and estate plans, otherwise we will not be included in their plans. Personal planning can occur at any time; so we need to ensure that there is ongoing awareness of Planned Giving opportunities in the parish and that resources are available to respond to donor requests.

While we need to maintain awareness, we also need to recognize that we are dealing with very personal issues. On the one hand, it is vitally important that we fit ongoing awareness of Planned Giving into the context of each parish and congregation. On the other hand, we need to confront the reluctance of many Anglicans to be direct about such matters. If we shy away from talking about Planned Giving, our members will be responding to the myriad of charities that have no such hesitation.

This chapter is intended to give you some ideas about what needs to be communicated and how you might go about it. As each parish and congregation is different, it is best that you put together your own "marketing strategy" for Planned Giving. *Planned Giving is a ministry, not a campaign.* Its success depends on a well-thought-out program that continues to remind and encourage people to be conscientious stewards of their accumulated assets.

What Do We Need to Tell People?

1. *What is Planned Giving?*
   Many people have only a vague notion about Planned Giving. People need to understand what it is, how it works, and why it is important to them and to the church.

2. *How does Planned Giving fit with the annual stewardship campaign and budget?*
   Simply stated, it doesn't! Planned Giving is part of our overall Christian stewardship, but it works on a different time scale (long term), deals with our assets rather than our income, and is concerned with funding the growth of our Christian ministry rather than meeting our current expenses.

3. *Why is Planned Giving important to the donor?*
   Stewardship of our accumulated wealth is a Christian responsibility. For more information, please see chapter 1, "A Theological Framework for the Life of Christian Stewardship" and chapter 11, "Planned Giving: A Theological Framework."

   Many North Americans do not have wills. If they die without a will, the government decides how their estate is to be distributed. Raising Planned Giving in the context of overall estate planning may prompt some people to attend to this important matter.

4. *Why is Planned Giving important to the church?*
   Planned Giving provides funding for activities that expand the ministry of the church and ensure its vitality in the future. In addition, each parish should have specific goals for new programs and growth that fit within Planned Giving.

5. *What is the Planned Giving program in the parish?*
   Legitimacy: that is, how Planned Giving is supported by the rector, parish council, etc.
   Organization: the role of the Planned Giving representative, and links to the parish council, the rector, etc.
   Diocese: how your program supports, and is supported by, the diocesan Planned Giving program.

6. *The types of Planned Giving opportunities*
   Most people do not think beyond bequests. It is important to the thinking of potential donors to introduce the various other ways of making a Planned Gift.

7. *Where donations can go and how they are used*
   Inform potential donors about the parish endowment or trust funds, the Episcopal Church ministries foundation of the diocese, the various funds of the national church, the Presiding Bishop's World Relief and Development Fund. The message is that there are lots of choices to meet specific donor interests and/or needs.

8. *How the money is protected*
   This is extremely important, particularly because of the financial issues for many parishes, dioceses, and the national church arising from residential schools. Donors need the assurance that their funds will be well managed in the long term and that they will be used for their intended purposes. Details of how the funds are established and managed should be available to those who ask.

9. *Success stories (as available) of the use of Planned Gifts*
   Tell the parish what is being accomplished with Planned Gifts. This is the best marketing tool you will have. Success breeds success. Demonstrating the use of funds to meet long-term goals will build confidence in our ability to be responsible financial stewards. It will take some time to get to the story-telling stage in the parish. Until then, share some diocesan stories or stories from parishes that have had an earlier start.

From Scarcity to Abundance

10. *Who to contact for more information*

The rector, as there will be some who are uncomfortable talking to a lay member of the parish on such a personal issue.

You, the Planned Giving representative for the parish.

11. *Donor recognition*

For some donors, recognition of their Planned Gift is a significant motivator. Depending on your parish culture, public recognition of Planned Gifts may be very appropriate, always with the donor's permission.

The Society of the Magi

One example of the type of recognition that is proven effective comes to us from the Episcopal Diocese of New York. The diocese has established the Society of the Magi, a society to recognize donors. Recognition not only thanks people for their extraordinary gift, it also helps maintain an ongoing relationship with the donor. We know that people who make a Planned Gift, or give to a Capital Campaign, are good candidates to make another gift. A person becomes a member of the society by making provision for the support of a congregation or other agency of the church through what are generally accepted as Planned Gifts. A lovely certificate is presented to members of the society each year at a diocesan reception.

How Do You Tell Our Story?

Remember, we are looking for the long haul, not a big, one-time, splashy campaign. Also, remember we are dealing with very sensitive, personal matters. Consider some of the following:

- talking about Planned Giving from the pulpit or front of the church periodically;

- distributing a parish Planned Giving brochure in display racks, with newsletters, in a service bulletin, and as part of the annual stewardship literature;

- displaying any diocesan Planned Giving brochures;

- conducting or arranging for workshops on estate planning, wills, end of life decisions;

- including a short "commercial" in the service bulletin at least once a month (see appendix 5 for some ideas on wording);

- running a series of articles on Planned Giving in the parish newsletter (see your diocesan web site from time to time for ideas, and share your ideas on the web site too);

- mentioning from the pulpit success stories on the use of donations to expand ministry in the parish;

- personal contact by the rector, the national church or diocesan Planned Giving director, or the Parish Planned Giving Representative, with key parishioners who are felt to be receptive to a personal approach;

- a regular report on donations, income, and the use of endowment or trust funds. Growth in funds will attract more donations. Demonstrating financial responsibility and openness will lessen fears of mismanagement;

- encouragement for parishioners who have made decisions on Planned Giving to offer personal testimonies;

- if it fits the parish culture and donor wishes, a celebration of Planned Gifts when they are received. Also, consider an "honor list" of those who have made gifts or included the church in their wills.

What Help is Available to You?

1. National church planned giving office (phone 800-697-2858).

2. The national church planned giving web page at
   http://www.episcopalfoundation.org/giving/givehome.html
   The Internet: for example, using Google search engine, try enter-
   ing "Christian Planned Giving" and "Planned Giving."

3. Diocesan brochures and resource people where available.
   The Episcopal Diocese of Texas, for example, has a planned giving link at http://www.epicenter.org/legac/shtm

PART FOUR

PARISH CAPITAL CAMPAIGNS AND FUND-RAISING FOR SPECIAL PROJECTS

17

Assessing Feasibility

From time to time in parishes major projects are necessary to position the congregation to do its ministry in the community into the future. In my stewardship ministry I occasionally get asked to consult with parishes as they consider undertaking significant Capital Campaigns. The million-dollar question always asked up front is simple: "Will we be successful and raise the money we need to fund our project?" The answer is not so simple. This is essentially what a feasibility study is designed to address.

As the stewardship volunteer in your parish, you can take a leading role to ensure that a reliable feasibility study or self-assessment exercise is undertaken. Surprisingly, you can complete a quality self-assessment exercise in-house, without spending money on high-priced fund-raising consultants. It takes a bit of time, some digging, and good cooperation from the envelope secretary and rector, but it isn't overly difficult to do.

A feasibility study or self-assessment exercise can save a parish a lot of pain and grief by asking the right questions *if* the leadership makes the commitment to listen to what the study reveals. Like sports teams that decide not to pull the trigger on a big trade, the best campaigns are sometimes those that don't happen or are delayed until the timing is right.

Two Key Indicators of Potential Campaign Success

We can narrow feasibility down to two factors that are most indicative of success in parish capital fund-raising campaigns. These factors are

1. Is there widely held *capacity* to give?

2. How *compelling* is the reason to undertake the project?

Experience shows that people with a capacity to give will take ownership of a project if the reason is compelling. Without that ownership, Capital Campaigns can fall well short of desired objectives. In most fund-raising situations, to adequately address these two questions, a self-assessment exercise must include many or all of the following issues:

- success of past Capital Campaigns;

- participation levels in previous campaigns;

- average gift levels in previous campaigns;

- number and size of major gifts in past campaigns;

- other (secular) campaigns that will be running concurrently in the parish's local catchment area;

- any peculiarities or issues in the local economy;

- types of projects the parish has historically been willing to fund;

- other financial demands on donor prospects;

- time elapsed since last major campaign targeted this donor base;

- capacity to give in current donor prospect base;

- appeal of various elements of a potential Case for Support;

- qualitative feedback on various messages that may be presented to donor prospects;
- level of support among influential parish opinion leaders.

Some of this work requires merely digging into past campaign records and analyzing the data. Other feasibility work involves analyzing current donor behavior from the parish list and pulling together some central messages for review with key donors and parish opinion leaders. At some point it will be necessary to conduct personal interviews with major donor prospects and opinion leaders to assess both the key indicators.

Chart of Giving Standards

One handy device I have used to determine capital fund-raising feasibility is to complete a parish chart of giving standards. This chart is intended primarily as a review of donor capacity to give and assumes that the main message of the campaign is going to be compelling. For a $300,000 campaign in a parish with 150 envelope holders, a giving standards chart could look like this:

Gift Amount	No. of Gifts	Total Dollars	Cumulative Dollars
$25,000	4	$100,000	$100,000
$15,000	3	$ 45,000	$145,000
$10,000	5	$ 50,000	$195,000
$ 5,000	5	$ 25,000	$220,000
$ 3,000	15	$ 45,000	$265,000
$ 1,000	35	$ 35,000	$300,000
TOTALS	67	—	$300,000

% Participation 44.7% (67 divided by 150)

Parish leadership doesn't just invent this chart out of thin air. It is arrived at by using all the questions reviewed earlier and in close consultation with the parish rector and envelope secretary. Educated guesses, based on historical and anticipated donations at each level, must be made to determine capacity to give and expected participation at each level. Use of the chart must be flexible. For instance, leadership may learn of a potential $100,000 gift and adjust the remainder of the chart accordingly.

If leadership looks at past parish Capital Campaigns and sees a historical participation level of 30% of households over three previous campaigns dating back twenty-five years, it is then not prudent to plan a campaign where 45% participation is needed for success—that is, unless there are unusual factors at play. Also, if it becomes apparent that four major gifts of $25,000 are needed for success and that there are only two donors with this capacity, then perhaps a more modest target should be contemplated.

One rule of thumb in secular fund-raising is that you have to ask for three major gifts in order to get one successful response at the major gift level. I suspect that this rule is a little conservative for church fund-raising, which may be closer to 2.5 requests for every major gift success, but you need to be aware of this dynamic because it may be indicative of your parish situation.

Capital fund-raising is an art, not a science. If, when you look at the chart, the target seems too aggressive, this *may* be a signal to parish leadership that the proposed project may be overly ambitious, and a scaled-back project may be more appropriate. These are difficult decisions. I have found the chart a very good starting point for assessing achievability of a target. Once you decide to move forward with a campaign, the chart of giving standards becomes a blueprint for executing the campaign and determining "ask" amounts during in-home visits with donor prospects.

The other key element of a self-assessment exercise or feasibility study is to obtain feedback from key donor prospects and opinion leaders. The purpose of these contacts is twofold. First, it gives you direction on how compelling your message or project is in the eyes of those who will have to support it. At this stage, donor prospects will tell you which elements of the proposed project are most appealing. This is a signal to the campaign committee to emphasize these components in any campaign promotional material.

Different donors are motivated by, and have a passion for, different aspects of a new ministry enabled by the project. It is very helpful to do a sounding of which elements of the project have the most widespread support. Often your committee will intuit the answers to this question. This doesn't negate the need to hear opinions directly from donors and to design materials accordingly.

The second key element is to obtain a sense of whether the key stakeholders will invest in the campaign at levels necessary to indicate success. If there is a major gap in the campaign message you wish to present, the self-assessment will usually tell you that something isn't resonating with donors. Often small working committees get too close to a project and don't see the logical flaws or shortcomings in the message. Feedback at this stage, before a campaign is launched, is helpful in ironing out any communications challenges and re-working the message to donors to maximize its impact.

In church-land, donors want to know how significant capital expenditures will truly make a parish better able to do ministry. An inner core, who are intimately acquainted with a building and its limitations, usually has no trouble viewing capital investment as necessary. However, my experience is that, outside the inner core, most people in the pews assume that the building is adequate to do any kind of ministry and have to be shown otherwise during the campaign.

Once you have feedback on your message, you will want to obtain feedback on willingness to invest in the campaign. In informal face-to-face interviews we then tell donors that we are testing the waters to see if our campaign is viable. We ask them whether they personally think they will donate to the campaign at significant levels. Then we listen. I have seen some parishes do this step by telephone, but I would advise against it. Those conducting the assessment really need to discern parishioner reaction—by studying body language and inviting the kind of questions that personal contact can elicit—so they know that respondents aren't just telling the committee what they think it wants to hear.

All the data gathered as part of this process then needs to be summarized and discussed among the parish leadership. From here, how you proceed depends largely on your local parish culture. You may want to use the dissemination of your feasibility data as an opportunity to foster further excitement for the project among the second tier of parish leaders. Call a special parish council, and share your learning from the self-assessment exercise or feasibility study. Many of these people will have been approached for input as respondents in the study. This is the chance to give them feedback.

After doing this work and obtaining input, you will have a good indication of whether it is wise to move forward with your capital project and fund-raising campaign. Then the fun begins!

18

The Importance of Praying the Capital Campaign

This is a tiny little chapter but vitally important. Scripture clearly shows that, before every significant event in his ministry, Jesus spent time in prayer. Before selecting the disciples, he went away to pray. Before feeding of the five thousand, he entered into prayer. Before turning his face to Jerusalem, he went off to pray. Before his arrest, Jesus sought time alone with the Father in Gethsemane.

It probably goes without saying that we need to create intentional time to seek God's will in determining whether a campaign is an appropriate way for a parish community to respond to the gospel, *before* we begin. Capital Campaigns can be very stressful and disruptive of parish life. No one takes them lightly. A time of prayer and reflection needs to drive the process. Prayer should be at the forefront of a campaign for many reasons, not the least of which is the self-care of the campaign team. Donors also want to know that parish leaders are grounded in prayer before contemplating a campaign.

Clearly, every Capital Campaign must be based on a strong theological framework. Parish leaders need to have utilized the discipline of theological reflection before taking a parish into a large project. If campaign committee members have done the theological reflection exercise, they will also be more invested in, and passionate about, the project because they will know that it is grounded theologically. Theological reflection on a campaign will be as different as the people

From Scarcity to Abundance

involved, but it may include asking the following questions or ones like them.

1. *Where is God in our plans?*
   If God is in something we are involved in, we can move forward in confidence. In Jeremiah 29:11–13 God instructed the Israelite exiles, "For surely I know the plans I have for you ... plans for your welfare and not for harm, to give you a future with hope."

2. *What does the gospel call us to do, to be the church in this place at this time?*
   This question involves reflection on both the individual and corporate response of the church, both to the gospel and a thorough assessment of local needs in the wider community. In a compelling Capital Campaign the parish has considered local needs assessment at length before moving forward. Projects provide an opportunity to parishes and individuals to become co-creators with God of the coming Reign of Christ.

3. *How will both the parish and the giver be blessed by the giving that will take place?*
   As campaign team members you are providing a ministry by giving donors an opportunity to give. It is in the genius of God that we are blessed as much by giving as by receiving. Reflection on how these blessings are already manifesting themselves is a valuable spiritual exercise for a parish.

Some Campaign Prayers

Here are a few prayers from a recent diocesan Capital Campaign in Niagara to stimulate your thinking.

Gracious God, we thank you for the plans you have made for our lives, individually and as a parish. We look to you in these days, believing that you have promised us a future and a hope. Fill our hearts with joy in believing, and help us to respond in the light of your faithful promises. Amen.

Loving God, we thank you for your gifts of grace and generosity: the grace that led Jesus to the cross, and that leads us, by faith in his cross, to the riches of forgiveness and salvation. Move our hearts, by your Holy Spirit, to such joyful thanksgiving that we may have the grace to give because Jesus gave. Amen.

Eternal God, I want my giving to be an expression of love for you. I unreservedly give all that I am and all that I have to you. I entrust my life to you. Let everything that comes from my life be pleasing to you and a blessing to others, for truly you love all people. Amen.

Dear God, it is wonderful that my gift could support our parish ministry and contribute to the care and blessing of this world. Help me to make a careful assessment of the way I invest my money. Give me a cheerful heart in giving, and let the resulting harvest be great for you. Amen.

Almighty God, thank you for the vision and invitation of the church to participate in this campaign. Give wisdom to our rector and parish leaders who will make choices to use campaign funds according to your will. Keep them and us vigilant in prayer, so that, according to your will, these funds will bear fruit in the lives of your people. Amen.

From Scarcity to Abundance

19

Creating a Compelling Message to Take to Donors

Jesus said: "Everyone then who hears these words of mine and acts on them will be like a wise man who built his house on rock. The rains fell, and the floods came, and the winds blew and beat on that house, but it did not fall, because it had been founded on rock." (Matthew 7:24–25)

In my previous career with a large multinational advertising agency, I learned a valuable lesson that is equally valid in the church. Executing a new advertising campaign is relatively easy, but all the creative genius in the world cannot rescue a project (or product) that is strategically unsound upfront. As a consultant, I can come into your parish and qualify donors, develop great material, train and motivate visitors, and put together a communication plan to maximize donor awareness for the length of a campaign. But if the message we are taking to donors is not compelling, we might as well have built our house on sand.

In many parishes, the success of a Capital Campaign is won or lost before the first visit ever happens. That's a bold statement but not far from the reality of capital fund-raising in the Anglican Church of Canada and Episcopal Church in the United States. Sadly, many parishes find out that their campaign was built on sand only by executing a campaign and failing. Either they lack the expertise or fail to take time to do a proper self-assessment exercise, or they neglect to find a way to make their message more persuasive when a study points out inadequacies in the message.

I have also seen campaigns founder because a small leadership group was so highly invested in the project that they failed to realize that the rest of the parish did not share their enthusiasm. The wider parish had not bought into the vision that the small leadership core was trying to articulate. Do not fall victim to these common traps before you even get your campaign underway.

When I first sit down with parish leaders, I always ask them informally to describe why the project is necessary. If in a face-to-face conversation five passionate leaders cannot explain to me succinctly and clearly why a project is necessary (and motivate me to get involved), then there is a huge problem. How can we expect donors to catch the excitement from mere promotional materials if the most passionate people involved in the project can't "sell" its necessity one-on-one?

In a Capital Campaign a convincing message to donors must include several components:

- a sound theological framework—how does this project respond to the gospel call to be the church at this time in this place?;
- an explanation of why the campaign is absolutely necessary and no other reasonable (that is, less expensive) alternatives to the project exist;
- a vision of how parish life will be significantly different when the project is complete;
- a vision of how people's lives will be impacted or changed by the new ministry that the project will enable;
- a reminder of how this project fits synergistically with the mission statement of the parish;
- a detailed timetable for the project;
- concrete specifics of how *all* the money raised will be spent;

- a plan for how any new programming will be sustained on an ongoing basis once operational;

- reassurance that donations will be spent wisely and well managed;

- a non-technical explanation of how the project will be financed and whether bridge financing will be necessary if the fund-raising includes a pledge campaign.

Essentially donors want to know:

- Why now?

- Why this?

- Why this much money?

- Why me?

Okay, I am only slightly kidding about the "why me?" part, but people need to know the answers to these questions to make an informed decision. All joking aside, the "why me?" question is really implicit. Donors need to be reminded of the baptismal call to be good stewards of their resources. For many in your parish, this will include their financial support of the campaign.

I tell parish leaders that a compelling message must paint a picture of their vision. You might wish to view this as dreaming a future or, in today's world, figuratively "making a video" to help donors visualize the dream. Donors need help imagining the future you want them to imagine. We don't ask them to donate $100,000 for lighting, paving, pavement marking, and drainage for the back parking lot. We ask them to imagine a new circular drop-off at the front door, volunteers in orange vests directing traffic on a busy Sunday morning, a golf-cart shuttle taking elderly people right to the front door. Maybe the rector is on the golf cart sneaking out for a game, but you get the idea.

We don't just tell donors that we need new meeting rooms. We dream about what new ministries we could empower if we had more space. We talk about the groups that we have had to turn away because we couldn't provide space for them to meet. We are always inviting donors to catch a vision.

Do you know the key "hot buttons" Episcopalian and Canadian Anglicans respond to? Can insights into these "hot buttons" fit into your message to donors? Anglicans can get very excited about the following ministries and get behind projects that sponsor them. In no particular order, the ministries that seem to touch Anglican donors deeply include

- expanded youth and children's programming;
- outreach projects to people in need;
- evangelism and hospitality;
- expanded pastoral care programming;
- church growth programs that will boost attendance;
- music enhancement campaigns;
- and finally, building maintenance and expansion where expansion empowers significant new ministry initiatives.

How many of these elements fit seamlessly into your parish's Case for Support? It is the Case for Support that becomes the foundation document of the campaign. All campaign promotional materials are culled from the Case for Support.

I recommend that the person in charge of writing the campaign Case for Support take the opportunity to interview several people in the parish whose ministries will be positively impacted by the project. The key question that needs to be asked and the question donors are asking is, *How will this project facilitate a major improvement of our ministry?*

To design a persuasive message to donors, the author needs to learn firsthand how the project is going to make a significant difference in the life of the parish. This compilation of stories then becomes the substance of the case. One thing that these interviews do is to provide juicy quotes, without which campaign materials tend to be impersonal and non-engaging.

Two key questions are often helpful in developing your message to donors:

1. What is it about our parish that would make donors commit to a notable gift?

2. How can we stress that this project is about giving to the parish and not to a campaign?

Have you ever been to lunch with friends who talk solely about themselves for an entire hour? It gets tedious, and you start to feel disconnected halfway through the meal. One common trap is to create campaign material that talks entirely about the parish and not about the donor. Ask yourself how you can shift the focus off the church and on to the interests of prospective donors. Your parishioners have passions—whether addressing the ills of society, leaving a legacy that will define what their life is about, or sustaining an institution that has been a part of the very fabric of their lives. Tap into those passions as you hone your campaign message. Remember that any campaign is always only a means to an end.

Finally, a compelling message must include a clear invitation to participate—a simple point but occasionally overlooked. Donors are created in the image of God. They have a God-given need to give and, through their givings, to work with you in partnership with God as co-creators of the New Jerusalem here on earth.

Instilling Donor Confidence

When I was working for the advertising agency I learned another valuable lesson. Clients would not entrust us with multimillion dollar advertising budgets until we showed them that we could handle day-to-day issues with competence. No matter how persuasive your campaign message is, donors will not invest in a project unless they have a high level of confidence in parish leadership.

Donors want to have confidence in the leadership on several levels. They do not want to entrust the campaign team with a major capital budget unless the leadership shows that it can manage the everyday parish operating-budget effectively. Donors want to know that campaign financing-projections have been well thought through and that leadership has properly calculated the potential bridge financing liability. They need to know that a project has been thoroughly costed out; they want transparency from parish leaders on such issues as building details, tendering process, allowance for incidentals; and they want assurance that contingency funds and plans have been considered.

Today's sophisticated donors need to know that investment performance and past management of endowments has been competent. When this kind of confidence has been displayed to donors, they are comfortable with investing in a campaign.

20

Delivering a Quality Invitation

During dinner hour on a Monday evening the doorbell rings. You back away from the table and walk to the door, wondering who could be disturbing your meal at this hour. On your doorstep is a canvasser from a local charity dedicated to helping middle-aged men unable to reach down and tie their shoes. The canvasser has been walking up and down the street knocking on every door and looks dejected from the lack of enthusiasm and concrete success. He is glad to find someone who has at least opened the door.

"I'm canvassing to help raise funds for home nursing to help men bend down and tie their shoes," he blurts out almost apologetically, his eyes transfixed on the smear of ketchup on your chin. Now, if you are in a lousy mood, suffering from indigestion, or have had a bad day at the office, you politely slam the door in his face. If the canvasser is lucky, you know a family member who has suffered through this devastating disability (or you yourself have experienced it). So, assuming he won't leave without a donation, you find yourself actually considering a gift.

The canvasser starts to get nervous during the moments of silence and, guessing that you are wondering what others on the street have given, he offers a suggestion. "Most people give $10," he tells you. So you reach into your pocket and flip the guy $10 in order to get a charitable tax receipt and get rid of him so that you can go back to the dinner table and finish your buffalo burger and fries.

Unwittingly, you have played out a dynamic not dissimilar from what happens all too often in parish Capital Campaign living room visits. Let's analyze this visit. The little exchange between the homeowner and the canvasser contains many of the key mistakes that parish visitors make during Capital Campaigns. Here are some reasons why:

- there is no or limited pre-visit communication between the visitor and the donor prospect to ensure the timing of the visit is convenient;

- the visitor's demeanor and body posture convey a sense that he is apologetic about being there and reveal that he probably believes deep down that he shouldn't be asking you for money;

- our imaginary visitor is actually afraid of asking directly for money;

- the visitor mumbles out why he is there but never actually delivers an invitation to give;

- the visitor assumes that the donor prospect is already familiar with the organization, its mission, and need without actually verifying this fact;

- nothing is presented to the donor prospect about the urgency of the need, and no reason to give is articulated;

- the visitor does not ask the donor prospect if he has any questions about the charity or this particular fund-raising drive;

- no information is provided on how the money will be used by the charity;

- the donor is not given a sufficient specific amount as a suggested gift and, therefore, defers virtually to a lowest common denominator;

- the visitor is uncomfortable in the silence and speaks while the donor prospect is thinking out what he should do;

From Scarcity to Abundance

- the visitor doesn't take the opportunity to tell the homeowner why he is canvassing and, therefore, misses the chance to explain his passion for the charity and its mission.

Some things were done right in this visit:

- the visit was face-to-face and therefore, by its very nature, personal;

- a context was offered for the amount to give (even if the context did not stretch the donor's philanthropic mindset);

- a gift was made!

We all know that virtually no training is given to the many secular charitable canvassers that knock on our front doors. Usually an area captain is assigned to a neighborhood and tries to find one person on each street to do canvassing. That person is handed a kit with receipts, brochures, and a deadline for finishing the street.

Your project is too important to take training lightly. This manufactured scenario highlights the importance of thorough, detailed visitor training. Once we get to this stage of the campaign, the focus becomes how best to issue a quality invitation to donors. After that, the donor's decision is a matter for the Holy Spirit and not the campaign committee.

Options for Asking for Support of the Campaign

Once you have your message and promotional materials complete, your donor list qualified, and your "ask amounts" established, it is time to invite donor prospects to invest in the project. Secular fundraising theory argues that two elements are non-negotiable essentials in a quality invitation:

1. making a face-to-face personal invitation;

2. asking the donor for a *specific* "stretch" amount.

Philosophically, I endorse any solicitation method that contains both of these two components. Let's review some of the more common ways of asking for Capital Campaign gifts and pledges.

An Every-Member Visitation

In this scenario, the parish list is usually broken down into three phases based on size of the "ask amount." These phases go under different names: advance phase, main phase, and general phase. The advance phase is usually the top 10% to 20% of the parish's identifiable givers list; the main phase is the middle 60 to 70% of the list; and the general phase is the remainder of identifiable givers. Donor prospects are assigned to a phase at a confidential "prospect review meeting" attended by the campaign chair, the rector, the envelope secretary, and the campaign fund-raising consultant (if applicable). Because of the confidentiality of this meeting, attendees are kept to a small "need-to-know" group.

Depending on the size of the parish, visitors are recruited and assigned approximately five to seven visits each. Ideally visitors make their calls in two-person teams, although this is not always feasible. Visitors are trained at the start of each phase, and the campaign is executed over a period of two to six months, again depending on the size of a parish. At the visitor training that kicks off the subsequent phases, visitors from the previous phase report on success.

Agendas for these training sessions typically cover the following areas of the campaign:

- an inspirational talk is given by the rector or the campaign chair about why they feel passionate about the campaign and why it is important to the parish;

- visitors are thanked profusely for their willingness to be part of the exciting project;

- the key messages of the Case for Support, and the reasons why the project is necessary at this time, are explained;

- a hands-on review of the campaign materials is given, to familiarize visitors;

- a review is offered of frequently asked questions that the visitor can expect on the visit;

- an explanation is given of the financial elements of the campaign: how much the project will cost, how donations will be spent, what the financing charges are, etc.

- a timetable for the project and the campaign is explained to visitors;

- the chart of giving standards is shown and the target for the campaign explained so that visitors understand how gifts at various levels fit into the overall campaign plan for success. Visitors are shown how to use the chart in a visit;

- visitors are formally invited to make their own gift in the training meeting;

- the steps of the call are explained and modeled by the trainer;

- visits are role-played and visitors get a chance to be both visitor and visitee;

- the visitor is taught how the pledge card is completed and how to introduce it into the visit (for a sample campaign pledge card, see appendix 6);

- visits are assigned;

- visitors are handed out personalized kits containing sufficient promotional materials and pledge cards with return envelopes; the chart of giving standards for the campaign; a sheet with the name, address, phone number, and "ask amount" for each household that visitor is assigned;

- expectations for reporting on progress are articulated to visitors;

- a general question and answer period is also highly recommended, so that visitors have a chance to vent their anxiety, be reassured, and also voice any remaining concerns they have.

As you can see, the training event is a lengthy meeting. Three hours is not uncommon because of the importance of training, the need to do role-playing, and the assignment of visits. I recommend that training take place immediately before visiting is to begin. It is wasting effort to train visitors weeks before the visitation. They need to put their training into effect right away, while it is still fresh in their minds.

Steps of the Call in an Every-Member Visitation

When I train visitors, I usually get them to think of their visit as having three main segments:

1. explanation of the project and its importance to the future of the parish;

2. a time for the donor to ask any questions and obtain clarification on the scope and essence of the project;

3. the "ask" for a specific "stretch amount."

The first segment should take approximately twenty minutes. After some small talk the visitor will find a way that works for them to segue into a discussion of the campaign. Since a project is usually complex and layered, and time is limited, it is impractical to both discuss the entire project and keep the visit to a reasonable time length. I encourage visitors to find an element of the project that they feel particularly passionate about. I invite them to talk about that element and to let their passion and enthusiasm become evident to the donor. And I suggest that they might say something like, "This is what I feel really passionate about in this project, and I know that, when you take the time to learn more about the project, you will find aspects of it that will stir your passions too!" Then I trust that this will happen.

The second segment is really controlled by the visitee. Depending on how many questions they have or what concerns they raise, the visitor will know when it is time to move to the "ask amount." The key at this point is to listen attentively. The donor will give clues about his or her possible level of commitment, and we need to listen for those clues.

The hardest part for most visitors is the third step—asking for a specific gift. Most visitors imagine horror stories of donors throwing tantrums when they are asked for a gift at a level with which the visitor is personally uncomfortable. It helps when visitors can explain that actually being a visitor means that they have already made their own commitment to the campaign.

Still, I wouldn't be surprised if 60% to 70% of visitors hesitate to speak out the desired "ask amount" at the moment of truth. Because of this understandable resistance, I have altered the training in parishes where visitors tell me they will have trouble. I suggest that, if they can't say the amount out loud, they point to a figure on the chart of giving standards and ask the donor to consider a gift at that level. The second most difficult task is then to remain silent while the donor processes what they have just been asked to consider.

If you are executing a campaign and have visitors who are reluctant to ask for money, it is important to remember the following insight: In a campaign where the prospect review meeting has been managed well, *we never ask a donor for a gift that is going to significantly alter their current standard of living*. The donor will still go to Florida next winter, still take the family to lunch after church three times in a month, and still trade in the used car for a new one when ready, regardless of what they give to the campaign. Donors have capacity. Our challenge is to show them compelling reasons why they should give.

It is my experience that every decision to increase financial support of the church is the result of a process of ever deepening conversion. Remember too that in every visit the final decision to give is not the visitor's concern but the work of the Holy Spirit. After laying out the case and asking for the gift, the visitor asks the donor to complete a confidential pledge card. If the donor is not ready to make that decision or commitment, the visitor is trained to return at a later date with the card and get it filled in at that time.

Advantages of the every-member visitation are many:

- face-to-face personal invitations take place;

- the potential for that invitation to be of high quality is maximized by the attention paid to visitor training;

- segmenting of the parish list creates more focused early effort on those with the highest capacity to give, enabling campaign leaders to create momentum for the campaign and generate additional energy as the campaign progresses;

- gifts at the advance gift level are more frequent and larger;

- every-member visitation campaigns have a proven track record of delivering campaign targets!

There are some significant limitations to the effectiveness of this approach:

- for a large parish, upward of thirty to fifty visitors are needed, and this may be unattainable from a recruiting standpoint. If visitors wish to visit in two-person teams, this problem is further exacerbated;

- it is unreasonable to expect that all thirty to fifty visitors will do a quality job of explaining the need and asking for the gift;

- many visitors report that it is difficult even to get the donor prospect to agree on an appointment time, and the process is sabotaged up front;

- many visitors are able to handle most of the call but can't bring themselves to ask for a specific amount of money.

- often visitors will achieve the "ask amount" but then leave the pledge card with the donor, despite having been trained to take the completed pledge card with them. This oversight is proven to reduce participation levels;

- in medium and large parishes, it takes a long time to complete the campaign.

Despite these negatives, an every-member visitation is still the best proven way to execute a parish Capital Campaign and should be given the most consideration when planning a project. Only if the limitations of an every-member visitation are too stringent for a parish, would I consider a different campaign methodology.

Modified Every-Member Visitation

A modified version of the every-member visitation may be suitable for your parish. Modifications are limited only by your creativity. In a modified version only a portion of the identifiable givers receive personal visits. The remainder of the parish still receives an invitation to participate in the campaign. In a modified campaign, less labor-intensive ways of delivering an invitation are used.

In one parish I remember that had 650 families, an every-member visitation was out of the question, as enough visitors could not be recruited. I either had to come up with a different plan or do all 650 visits myself. This was not going to happen—the Stanley Cup playoffs were on at the time!

The parish list of givers was divided into three groups. The first tier of about 150 households was visited. The second tier of 300 families was divided into four groups, and each group was invited to one of four wine-and-cheese parties. A group presentation about the campaign was made, and attendees were handed a letter with a specific "ask amount," along with a brochure and a pledge card. The final tier of 200 "less committed" families received a brochure, a letter, and a pledge card in a direct mail campaign. They were asked to consider gifts of $1,000 or less.

Other parishes modify this recipe by doing in-home "group asks" at neighborhood parties. The intimate atmosphere provides an opportunity for a Bible study to set out a theological framework for the campaign. With this methodology, fund-raising can be executed on an accelerated schedule. The campaign is over sooner and, therefore, is less distracting and disrupting to parish life.

The committee sets up these meetings over the span of a month, and members make a face-to-face "ask" in the comfortable setting of a home, rather then in a big parish hall with seventy-five to a hundred people. These "group ask" situations are preferable to a mail invitation but have limitations too. Often donors don't feel safe about asking questions or articulating objections. As a result, the committee misses an opportunity to respond to concerns and, therefore, may fail to secure a gift, either large or small.

Remember that modified versions of the every-member visitation are primarily useful when visitor recruitment is a problem.

21

Communication During a Parish Capital Campaign

If you are going to have a Capital Campaign, you will need a communications plan for the various phases of fund-raising and construction, and the aftermath of the campaign.

I recommend that parish leadership observe the discipline of putting pen to paper and writing a communications plan. The exercise of making the plan will generate a wealth of communication ideas. It will also help to focus the committee on those communication needs that change as the campaign and the project that it funds progress. When writing a communications plan, three key questions need to be considered:

1. What are the messages we need to convey at each stage of the campaign?

2. What are the messages we need to convey at each phase of the project the campaign is funding?

3. Who is the target audience for each message?

Messages at Each Stage of the Campaign

Early in a campaign the communications thrust can assist the campaign in many ways:

- explaining the decision-making process to move forward with a project;
- outlining the vision and theological framework of the campaign;
- recruiting committee members and volunteers;
- announcing key training dates;
- announcing early success versus campaign goal as visits commence.

As the campaign progresses, the communications effort can assist in

- consulting with the project committee;
- keeping the campaign goal and the good news stories of donor support in front of the congregation;
- reminding donors to welcome visitors when they call and return pledge cards promptly;
- building excitement as the goal nears attainment.

In the final stage of the campaign communication is vital to

- keep visitors motivated to finish their visits;
- celebrate success as the target is achieved;
- create awareness of key dates as the parish project moves from concept to implementation.

Finally, it is extremely important to keep up communication after the campaign to tell donors how their money is being spent. This is where many communication efforts fail. Donors need to be reminded that their investment in the project and the parish is bearing fruit in people's lives, in order to motivate donors to complete their pledge long after the campaign is over. This effort should continue until the entire pledge period has been concluded. Without this focus, a campaign runs the danger of suffering serious slippage in donor pledge fulfilment.

Messages at Each Phase of the Project

As a parish (building) project begins to unfold, it is extremely important to plan the messages you wish the parish to receive. From preliminary approval stages to ceremonial ground-breaking to official grand opening, you want people to catch the excitement and feel ownership of the campaign and project.

I cannot overemphasize the importance of getting people on board with the project early! *Include the entire congregation in the initial decision-making process and keep them informed throughout the campaign.* The way we get people on board is through effective communication.

Strike a group including workers on both the campaign and the project, and brainstorm the messages that need to be communicated. Then brainstorm creative ways to communicate these messages, and draw up a communications plan. Assign a key communications contact person who will assume responsibility for executing the plan and ideas.

Use every vehicle at your disposal—bulletin boards, displays of models, newsletters, special newsflash one-page bulletins, pew leaflet handouts, vestry reports, e-mail blasts, web site updates. Two parishes that I worked with created fridge magnets showing an artist's conception of their new facilities, to keep the projects in front of people every day.

One cannot overestimate the importance of transparency and open communication during a project, and the direct correlation between thorough communication and eventual fund-raising success. I recommend that every parish appoint a communications chair and that the chair be an integral part of the campaign management team. This person is also a natural liaison with your building team (if the project involves building), as these two committees need to be talking to each other regularly.

Target Audience

Whether we are conscious of it or not, all communication is always tailored to a target audience. It is advisable to spend some effort considering who your target audience is for each element of your communications plan. That target audience *will* change. Some communication dispatches will be targeted at donors, some at campaign volunteers, some at other stakeholders (for example, community groups using your facility). Awareness of the importance of intentional targeting will maximize the effectiveness of your communications plan.

Branding Your Campaign and Project

Most parish campaigns have a catchy campaign slogan that reflects the essence of the project. I remember one diocesan campaign that we wanted to call "Leap of Faith." This slogan was scuttled when the bishop pointed out that many people would suggest he take a flying leap over the Niagara Gorge if he announced yet another diocesan campaign. But I still like that slogan. The primary objective of having a slogan is to give parishioners an easy handle for talking about the project. It should be short—just a few words—be easy to spell, and roll off the tongue easily.

The key to strong parish communication is to brand all communications and to be consistent in how you use the branding. It is essential to create a unique graphic visual identity and stick to it. Choose a font for your slogan and utilize that font every time you use the slogan. A cardinal sin in branding theory is to use different fonts in different materials. Resist this temptation.

Perhaps someone in your parish has graphic design talents or access to someone with this ability. If you can, arrange for the design of a logo, and use it in all communications materials. Don't mess with the logo once you have it designed. Use the same colours and size whenever you can. Include the logo on letterhead, in visitor's kits, at the top of pew bulletin announcements, in newsletters and newsflashes, on the parish web site and the campaign thermometer. Don't mess with other logos. Always treat the campaign name and slogan in a consistent manner. People will come to associate the logo with everything about the campaign, and it will, over time, trigger associations you wish to reinforce in the minds of donors and congregants.

Like fund-raising in general, communication is an art and not a science. I recommend factoring a reasonable budget for communications materials. Many promotional offerings from churches look as if they were printed in black and white on an old Gestetner duplicator. These materials make the organization look amateurish and unworthy of the donor's trust. Donors are being inundated with materials from secular not-for-profit organizations. These secular materials almost always incorporate sound graphic design, and are printed in four colors on glossy coated paper. The challenge is to make your materials look good while also nurturing the perception that the campaign committee is being a good steward of donor dollars.

Don't be timid. Taking into account the local community fund-raising environment, make your main campaign brochure a four-colour brochure. But you might use non-glossy uncoated paper to convey the message that you aren't blowing the bundle on expensive solicitation materials, while still looking competent and professional.

Have fun with communications. We tend to get serious in the church when it comes to these mega projects because they always seem to be of critical importance to a parish's long-term ability to do ministry. Maybe you can ask your youth group to produce a CD-ROM, write a rap song, or burn a DVD with the basic information on the project, the vision, and some stories of how the project will enrich parish life.

Get others involved and invested. Put the campaign logo on fridge magnets, postcards, pens, and paper. Sell stationary carrying the campaign logo. Hold a trivia contest with pertinent details about the project. Throw a pizza party with a tour of the site at different stages of construction. Insert a project update with the donor's annual pledge-reminder letter, and a little novelty (like the fridge magnet or a pre-printed notepad with logo) to keep the pledge commitment reminder in front of donors.

Donor Recognition

I was walking through Brock University in St. Catharines, Ontario, Canada, as we were given a tour of the 2004 General Synod facilities. Donor recognition plaques were everywhere. In one hallway eight benches had plaques announcing that the bench was a donation of Mr. or Mrs. Greenbucks. Every lecture hall, corridor, and drinking fountain displayed a plaque honoring the generosity of donors. (I believe the toilets were sponsored by American Standard!) Commemorating the outstanding male athlete of the year award was a permanent plaque bearing the name of a female donor as sponsor of the award. (I guess they couldn't find a male donor to recognize for that category.)

Depending on your local parish culture, it may be appropriate for you to recognize donor contributions to the financial campaign. Many will say that the recognizing of donors is counter-cultural in church-land. In the words of *MASH*'s Colonel Sherman Potter, "horse hockey." Just look at the stained glass windows in your church. In most parishes, chalices, fonts, tabernacles have engraved memorials on them. Perhaps three-quarters of the hymn books in the country bear bookplate memorials, and many parish halls across the land are named after a benefactor.

We can use donor recognition techniques to maximize campaign contributions. During one campaign I consulted with the parish to compose a price list for the recognition of major gifts. The parish hall could be named after a loved one for a gift of $250,000. The fireside room could be named for $75,000. (In this case the donor was contemplating $60,000 but increased the gift to take advantage of the memorial naming opportunity.)

I recommend that the campaign committee dedicate at least two meetings to formulating a donor recognition strategy for the campaign. You can sit down as a committee and consider gift-naming opportunities for donor recognition that mesh nicely with anticipated gifts on your chart of giving standards. You can also plan a wall with plaques containing the names of all donors to a campaign. Of course, you will want to make sure that a mechanism is in place to protect the privacy of any donor requesting anonymity.

A Final Word about Capital Campaigns

In all stewardship activities, whether annual pledging or Capital Campaigns, we cannot over-emphasize the importance of gaining the support of the clergy. All the hard work of planning and executing a campaign can be undone without the clear, unmistakable support of the clergy, especially the rector. *This includes clergy financial support of the campaign*. It's deadly in a Capital Campaign, for example, when the rector is asked how much he or she is pledging, then reluctantly responds or evades the question.

Donors' confidence level in the campaign is dramatically increased when they know that the rector is investing in the campaign too. This may be hard for some clergy to hear, but I am afraid it is a reality that can't be ignored.

A parish Capital Campaign is a huge undertaking. From a recruiting standpoint, I have found that it easier to recruit volunteers when they are told that the commitment being requested is for a finite period of time, and not an ongoing multi-year ministry.

When a campaign is well conceived and widely supported, few things in parish life can be as rewarding as taking part in a campaign that situates a parish to do its ministry for the next twenty-five year cycle. If you have read this far in this section of the manual, a Capital Campaign could be imminent in your parish. Good luck. May it be a blessing to you, and a time of personal and spiritual growth. On several occasions Capital Campaigns have gifted me in this way. I pray that you may receive that gift.

Questions for Consideration

1. Is there someone in your parish who is a communications professional, or who may be skilled at communications, and who would take a lead role in developing and executing a communication plan for your Capital Campaign?

2. Reflecting on the various memorials around the building, and on historical practice, what is your parish culture and policy around donor recognition?

3. How has this policy been communicated to the parish at large?

4. What naming opportunities exist with your parish project?

Appendix 1

Stewardship—Some Useful Resources

Resources for stewardship abound. As a matter of fact, they are overflowing. Here are a few web sites and books I hope you will find especially helpful.

Web Sites

Anglican Church of Canada Planned Giving resources
http://generalsynod.anglican.ca/ministries/departments/planned_giving/

Anglican Diocese of Niagara
Narrative Budgeting Power Point Presentation to help sell the concept to your parish leadership.
http://www.niagara.anglican.ca/financialdev/June%202004%20Parish%20Narrative%20Budget%20Presentation%20(2)_files/frame.htm

Planned Giving web site
http://www.niagara.anglican.ca/plannedgiving/plannedgiving.htm

Stewardship web site (especially for narrative budgeting)
http://www.niagara.anglican.ca/synodsteward.htm

Archdiocese of St. Louis (Roman Catholic) Children's Stewardship
http://www.archstl.org/stewardship/whatis/children.html

Ecumenical Stewardship Center
An excellent web site with some great ideas, a newsletter, and annual magazine.
www.stewardshipresources.org

Canadian Anglican stewardship cyber discussion group
A yahoo discussion group for Anglicans across Canada to share beliefs, experiences, and ideas about stewardship and legacy giving in their Christian life and faith. Members of the Evangelical Lutheran Church, the Episcopal Church in the United States, and our Anglican brothers and sisters in other parts of the world are welcome to join.
stewardshiplife@yahoo.ca

Episcopal Diocese of New York stewardship resources
http://www.dioceseny.org/index.cfm?Action=News.StewardshipNews

Evangelical Lutheran Church in America (ELCA) web site
Excellent resources.
http://www.elca.org/dcm/stewardship/

Also, spiritual gifts inventory and assessment tool with scriptural resources and self-administered assessment exercise.
http://www.elca.org/dcm/evangelism/assessments/assess4_spiritgifts.html

Evangelical Lutheran Church in Canada (ELCIC) web site
http://www.elcic.ca/steward/steward.html

Google search. Enter the words "spiritual gifts inventory" into the Google Internet search engine, and you will discover many excellent spiritual gift discernment and assessment tools.

St. Francis of Assisi (Roman Catholic) Parish, Wichita, Kansas
http://www.stfranciswichita.com/stewardship/development.
asp?f=home

Publications

Boers, Theo A. 2003. *Three Simple Rules.* Morris Publishing. Written from a Christian perspective, this book is focused on helping the reader understand and apply sound personal financial management principles. Send $5.00 US with your name and address to Three Rules, 2600 Five Mile Rd NE, Grand Rapids, MI 49525 or download free at http://www.threerules.org.

Foster, Richard J. 1981. *Freedom of Simplicity.* New York: HarperCollins, Publishers.
http://www.harpercollins.com/catalog/book_xml.
asp?isbn=0060628251

Gordon, David W. 1998. *A Plan for Stewardship Education and Development through the Year.* Toronto: Anglican Book Centre. Used in Niagara Diocese.
http://www.christianity-books.com/A_Plan_for_Stewardship_
Education_and_Development_
Through_the_Year_An_Outline_Manual_0819218030.html

Giving. A magazine published annually by the Ecumenical Stewardship Center, Indianapolis, Indiana. Worth the $7.00 US price for an annual parish subscription.
www.stewardshipresources.org

Nouwen, Henri J. M. Copyright 2004, Estate of Henri J.M. Nouwen. *The Spirituality of Fund-raising.* This booklet is available from <www.HenriNouwen.org>.

Roseman, Ellen. 2004–2005. *Money 101: Every Canadian's Guide to Personal Finance.* Mississauga, Ontario: John Wiley & Sons Canada, Ltd.

Schwarz, Christian, and Brigitte Berief-Schwarz. 2001. *The Three Colors of Ministry.* Natural Church Development Institute. A Trinitarian approach to identifying and developing your spiritual gifts. Available through the NCD web site at <http://www.ncd-international.org/BooksMinistry.html>.

Stanley, Thomas J., and William D. Danko. 1998. *The Millionaire Next Door.* New York: Pocket Books.

Appendix 2

An Exercise for Completing a Personal Stewardship Audit

Some Questions for Quiet Reflection

What is your earliest memory of money as a child? Your happiest memory?

What attitude did your mother have toward money? Your father? When was money discussed in your family as you were growing up?

Has your attitude toward money changed now that you are older? How?

Do you feel guilty about the money you have? Covetous of others who have more money than you? Does having or not having money affect your self-esteem?

How do you deal with the fact that we in Western culture live relatively comfortably while two-thirds of the people of the world are poor?

Draw a continuum line on a large piece of paper. The coordinate on the left is your birth and on the right, your death. Plot the key moments in your life when you gained significant learning about the place of money in your life. What was God doing in your life at those moments?

What kind of volunteer work do you find most satisfying or fulfilling? Why is that work fulfilling to you? How does your volunteering utilize your gifts and talents?

From Scarcity to Abundance

Appendix 3

Proportionate-Giving Worksheet

Proportionate giving means that shares of our personal resources of *time and talent and treasure* are being devoted to God's work on a regular schedule. It is a commitment made in response to the love that God has shown for us in Jesus Christ, as well as in the events of our daily lives. It is an offering of "ourselves, our souls and bodies."

The tithe is a standard by which we measure our offerings. All that we are and all that we have comes from God and still belong to God and is to be used for God's work and purposes in our world. Within that context, the biblical tithe (10%) becomes our goal in deciding what portion of our resources will be given.

This worksheet offers a means of determining your present level of support for the local church and establishing a commitment for the coming year. It is not to be returned to the church. It is intended for personal use with prayerful consideration in the privacy of your home.

I. To decide on your offering of *time and talent:*

Example: Your Schedule

Assuming a week of 168 hours (24 x 7),

	Example	*Time Spent*
1. Calculate the number of hours spent in work and sleep.	40 + 56 = 96	_____

	Example	*Time Spent*
2. Calculate the number of hours remaining.	168 – 96 = 72	_____
3. Consider giving *at least* the tithe (10%) of your time to God's work (in the church or beyond).	7 hours/week	_____

II. To decide on your offering of *treasure:*

First find your current level of financial support of your local church by dividing your *annual gift amount* by your *income* for the same period. (Use either gross income figures or net income figures.)

	Example	*Your Figures*
A. Current Income	$20,000	$_____
B. Current Annual Donation	$ 600	$_____
C. Current Percentage level (Divide line B by line A)	3%	_____%

From Scarcity to Abundance

III. A financial commitment for the coming year might be based on one of the following options:

	Example	Your Figures
A. *Tithing*		-
1. Expected Income	$ 21,000	$_____
2. The Biblical Tithe	10%	_____10%
3. New Commitment (Multiply line 1 by line 2)	$ 2,100	$_____

	Example	Your Figures
B. *Increasing the Present Level by 1%*		
1. Expected Income	$21,000	$_____
2. Current Percentage plus 1%	4%	_____%
3. New Commitment	$ 840	$_____

C. *Adopting the Church Goal*		
1. Expected Income	$21,000	$_____
2. Minimum Percentage Goal	4.5%	_____%
3. New Commitment	$ 945	$_____

A Sample Pledge Card
for an Annual
Stewardship Program

Commitment to the Ministry of St. Paul's Parish—2006

Name: _____

Telephone: _____

Street Address: _____

City: _____

State: _____ Zip Code: _____

In joyful thanksgiving for God's abundant blessings overflowing in my life I/We hereby declare my/our intention to commit to the ministry and mission of St. Paul's Anglican Church my offering of

1. The equivalent of _____ hours per week to the Lord's work in the parish;

2. Using my/our personal talents in the parish to support the ministries of _____ ;

3. My/Our financial support of parish ministry of $ _____ payable at a rate of $ _____ per week, month, or year (circle one).

Signed: _____

Date: _____
        day/month/year

Adapted from John D. Gordon, Christ Church, Seattle, WA.

Planned Giving Messages
for Sunday Bulletins

One generation plants the trees;
another gets the shade.

—Chinese Proverb

Please remember St. Simon's in your will.

Declare A Personal Jubilee

Remember St. James's in your will.

Declare Your Passion For The Lord

Remember St. John's in your will.

Give Through the Church to
Touch the Lives of People in Need

Remember St. Timothy's in your will.

How Do You Want To Be Remembered?

Remember St. Philip's in your will.

Pay It Forward
Declare a Personal Jubilee

Remember St. James's in your will.

Continue Your Caring

Your caring can live on through the thoughtful stewardship of your accumulated resources in a will. For more information, contact _____, your Parish Planned Giving Representative (123-456-7890).

Gifts That Give Back

Contact your Planned Giving Representative in our parish (_____ at 123-456-7890) for more information on giving a gift that not only gives to St. Andrew's, but also provides a source of income, peace of mind, and tax efficiency.

You Determine the Future

A will lets you, not the government, decide how your estate is used. Protect your family and what you value by making or updating your will now. Please remember St. Paul's in your thinking.

Appendix 6

A Sample Pledge Card for a Parish Capital Campaign

Commitment to the St. Elizabeth's "Leap of Faith" Campaign

[Campaign Logo]

Campaign Record

Visitor:_____ Date of Visit:_____

Name:_____ Telephone: _____

Street Address:_____

City:_____ State:_____ Zip Code: _____

To the honor and glory of God, and to help create a healthier, more vibrant, outward-looking parish I/We agree to pledge a gift of $ _____ payable over _____ years to the parish of _____ for the *"Leap of Faith"* Campaign.

Amount Enclosed: $ _____ Balance of $ _____

Balance to be paid ❑ Yearly ❑ Semi-Annually ❑ Quarterly ❑ Monthly

Beginning (date): _____

month/day/year

Signature(s):   _____ Date: _____

Signature(s):   _____ Date: _____

Payment Plan (Please check one plan)

❑ Pre-authorized automatic debits (Please complete reverse side and attach voided check)

❑ Post-dated checks (Please attach all post-dated checks)

❑ Periodic reminders (You will be mailed reminders according to the payment schedule chosen above)

❑ Monthly deduction from my VISA or other credit card (Fill out the reverse of this card as you would with a pre-authorized debit)

Thank you for your gift!

Please make checks payable to:

_____ Episcopal Church, *"Leap of Faith"* Campaign

Pre-Authorized Payment/ Credit Card—Authorization Form

I (We) hereby authorize the parish of _____ Anglican Church to draw on my (our) account with my (our) financial institution for the *"Leap of Faith"* campaign.

1.Pre-authorized Bank Withdrawal

Name of Bank: _____ Branch No. :_____

Account No.: _____ Type of Account: _____

Signature(s): _____

Date: _____ Date of First Debit: _____

month/day/year

Or

2. Pre-authorized Credit Card Monthly Debit

❑ VISA ❑ MasterCard ❑ Amex ❑ Discover

Name on Card: _____

Card No. :_____

Expiry Date:_____ Signature: _____

Date: _____ Date of First Debit: _____

month/day/year

Please remember to attach a voided check.

Appendix 7

22 Stewardship Preaching Tips

1. Stewardship preaching starts with a personal philosophy of pastoral care. If people know you care about them, they will listen. First and foremost, provide pastoral care.

2. All stewardship preaching comes from a basic premise: God is "the Great Giver," the creator and owner of all; we are the stewards.

3. From time to time, do the work of reflecting on your own theology of giving and sense of God's abundance and providential care in your life. *Allow your own sense of gratitude and blessing to come through in your preaching.*

4. We are a people of the story, which is why the narrative budgeting approach resonates. Reflect on, and then tell, your own stewardship story. People will listen.

5. Remember: people want to know how your own personal sense of stewardship of your baptismal ministry is part of the very fabric of your life. Help people to understand that it is through our stewardship of the gifts of God that we live out our baptismal promises.

6. When looking at lections keep in mind the many ways we are

called to be stewards. This will provide content for stewardship sermons. We are called to be stewards of

- creation/environment;

- our personal and work relationships;

- our personal health;

- our treasure;

- our spiritual gifts.

    For preachers we can add to this list

- the word; and

- the mission and ministry of the parish.

7. Stewardship preaching is *not* a once-a-year event. One of our challenges is to help parishioners look at life through a stewardship lens. When we reframe our own understanding, we can then teach others. Take a good look at the Diocese of Ontario RCL stewardship notes that can be found at <http://www.ontario.anglican.ca/resources.htm#stew >

Archdeacon Michael Pollesel of that diocese has written a few thoughts on how every week's lections can be viewed from a stewardship perspective. He has completed this exercise for all three years of the Revised Common Lectionary.

8. Use the Bible. From the very first book of the Bible, the image of God is one of an abundant, lavish giver. When we deny that we are created in God's own image, we are not allowing ourselves to become what God has made us to be. Look for biblical stories about gratitude and abundance. Remind parishioners that Jesus talked more about money than he did about heaven or prayer.

9. In the content of your sermons, invite lay people to take the time to share and reflect on their personal stories of God's care for them.

10. Encourage and find occasions to celebrate courage and risk that is informed by prayer. It takes courage to grow in Christian stewardship. It is a process and involves conversion and the work of the Holy Spirit. We are facilitators of that work.

11. Focus on outreach. A preacher's task is to help create a bigger vision of the world in which we live, to make people understand that being generous makes a difference in the world.

12. Talk of money in the church is within the context of "doing ministry," so you can be unapologetic.

13. Always invite others to give. People experience great joy in giving. People *need* to give.

14. Make it personal.

15. Encourage people to tithe their time. We all may not have the same financial resources, but we all have the same amount of time. If people move toward personal growth by tithing their time, they will naturally gravitate toward the use of their talents, and grow in commitment and deployment of their treasure.

16. *Never* shame people into giving.

17. Sometimes we don't stop to think that what we are preaching is a stewardship sermon. In some sense, every sermon we preach is a stewardship sermon, because every sermon we preach is about how we respond to God's grace in our lives.

18. Remember that you are not preaching to try to increase parish revenue but to transform lives. In this way we can be totally unapologetic. We are gifting our congregations by helping

them to see that their stewardship is an essential and life-giving part of their Christian discipleship.

19. Reflect on your audience. Most are probably struggling through life, locked in a personal spirituality of scarcity. They need comfort, hope, and the challenge to allow themselves to be transformed by the good news of God's abundant care. Others in your parish (a few) will spend more of their head space in a spirituality of abundance. They need affirmation and encouragement to reinforce that they are on the right track.

20. Think of your role as companion. As parish clergy we walk with our people through the roller-coaster ride of life. As a stewardship minister you may find it helpful to think of your role as companion on a journey from scarcity to abundance.

21. Thank people often for what they have done, what they are doing, and what they will do in the future.

22. Reflect on your own discomfort around preaching about money. Claim it. Own it. Then go out and experiment and have fun. *Good luck!*